D0712753

"Mixed Blood" Indians

THEDA PERDUE

"Mixed Blood" Indians

Racial Construction in the Early South

Mercer University Lamar Memorial Lectures No. 45

The University of Georgia Press   *Athens and London*

© 2003 by the University of Georgia Press
Athens, Georgia 30602
All rights reserved
Set in Berthold Baskerville by BookComp, Inc.
Printed and bound by Thomson-Shore
The paper in this book meets the guidelines for
permanence and durability of the Committee on
Production Guidelines for Book Longevity of the
Council on Library Resources.
Printed in the United States of America
07 06 05 04 03 C 5 4 3 2 1
Library of Congress Cataloging-in-Publication Data
Perdue, Theda, 1949–
"Mixed blood" Indians : racial construction in the
early South / Theda Perdue.
p. cm. – (Mercer University Lamar memorial lectures ;
no. 45)
Includes bibliographical references and index.
ISBN 0-8203-2453-1 (hardcover : alk. paper)
1. Indians of North America–Mixed descent–
Southern States. 2. Indians of North America–
Cultural assimilation–Southern States. 3. Race awareness
–Southern States. I. Title. II. Series.
E78.S65 P46 2002
975'.00497–dc21   2002007121

British Library Cataloging-in-Publication Data available

For George Tindall

Contents

Preface

In 1971 I was a law student at Mercer University. I found the repetitive nature of legal training to be mind dulling, so I decided to attend the Lamar Lectures delivered by George Tindall of the University of North Carolina. Published the following year as *The Disruption of the Solid South* (Athens: University of Georgia Press, 1972), Tindall's lectures focused on the role of race in southern politics. For the first time in my life, I heard someone discuss race academically, not as a fact of life, but as a social construct that served specific economic and political purposes. I suddenly became aware that race had a history and that its history had a great deal to do with the past and present South. As I listened to the lectures, I decided that I did not want to be a lawyer; I wanted to be George Tindall. I promptly quit law school and applied to graduate school in history. While my research has taken me into Native American history, the topic Tindall broached continues to have relevance for me. In these lectures, I explore race in a very different way than Tindall did, but he set me on this course.

In the eighteenth and early nineteenth centuries, many Europeans married Native women and had children whom whites called "half-breeds," a word now considered racist and derogatory and replaced by the presumably less offensive terms "mixed blood," "*mestizo*," or "*métis*." The large number of people of European ancestry

ix

who lived among southern Indians in the eighteenth century and their "mixed blood" offspring have contributed to the perception that these Native societies were more "civilized" than those of Native people elsewhere in North America. The assumption that the presence of "mixed bloods" made a society more "civilized" is problematic on several levels. For one, this assumption suggests that culture follows "blood," that is, that people of European descent behaved in certain ways, not because they had learned those behaviors, but because the behaviors were innate. Furthermore, even if we dismiss the notion of innate behavior, it implies that the culture of Europeans was stronger than those of Native people so that individuals of "mixed blood" were more likely to behave like the Europeans of their ancestry than like the Indians with whom they lived. And finally, it drives a wedge between the members of a Native community by using "blood" to privilege some individuals, to discredit others, and ultimately to racialize Native societies in ways that are foreign to Native cultural traditions. The time has come to move beyond a history of southern Indians that rests on "blood" as a primary category of analysis. In order to do so, we need to understand more fully the incorporation of non-Indians into Native societies, the participation of their descendants in tribal life, and the construction of the racial category of "mixed blood." These are the three topics I have addressed in this year's Lamar Lectures. Obviously, a volume of this length can only scratch the surface of a topic as complicated as racial construction, but we must begin to reconsider the way we think about Native elites in the early nineteenth century.

I would like to thank the Institute for the Arts and Humanities at the University of North Carolina, which awarded me a fellowship to work on these lectures. The generosity of J. Scott and Nancy Cramer of Winston-Salem, North Carolina, made the fellowship possible, and I am grateful to them and the many other private

donors who enhance research opportunities at public institutions.
I also received funding from UNC's research committee and the
Center for the Study of the American South. I appreciate the hard
work of my research assistants, Rose Stremlau and Cary Miller.
Claudio Saunt, Kathryn Braund, Karl Davis, Joe Anoatubby,
Rowena McClinton, James Taylor Carson, and Greg O'Brien pa-
tiently answered my antiquarian and genealogical queries about the
tribes on which they are experts. I especially appreciate Claudio's
professional friendship. We do not agree on much about southeastern Indians, but I have enormous respect for his intellect, and
the broader debate of which we are part greatly enriches the field.
Many conversations with graduate students have sharpened my
thinking on the issues raised in these lectures. In addition to Rose,
Cary, Karl, and Joe, who are mentioned above, I would like to
thank Victor Blue, Malinda Maynor, and Meg Devlin. As always,
my greatest intellectual and personal debt is to my in-house ex-
pert, Michael D. Green, who answered endless questions, loaned
me scores of books, and read countless drafts. Anna Smith, a fine
historian of the relationship between Moravians and Cherokees,
has been the kind of cheerleader every scholar wants and the kind
of friend every woman needs. Mike and Anna attended the Lamar
Lectures along with my mother Ouida Perdue, aunt Avis Bell, and
cousin Audrey George. Their presence made this an even more
memorable experience. At Mercer, Sarah Gardner, Michael Cass,
and their colleagues offered exceptional hospitality, and Bobbie
Shipley kept things running smoothly. I am grateful to all of them
and to the Lamar Lecture Committee, which gave me the opportunity after thirty years to *be* George Tindall.

"Mixed Blood" Indians

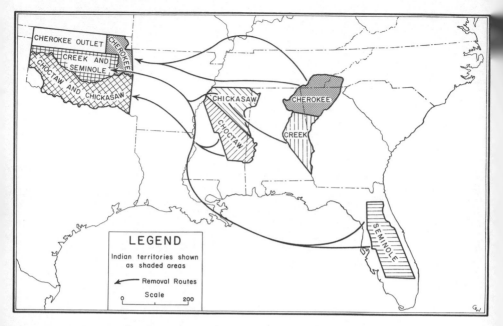

Southern Indian Nations before and after removal.

From *Nations Remembered: An Oral History of the Five Civilized Tribes*, ed. Theda Perdue.

CHAPTER ONE

"In the Indian Manner"

Natives and Newcomers
in the Eighteenth Century

In the late eighteenth century the famous naturalist William Bartram traveled extensively among the Creeks, Seminoles, and Cherokees. In addition to collecting botanical samples, Bartram wrote about the land he saw and the people he met. On his journey, Bartram encountered a variety of non-Natives, people of European and African ancestry, who made their homes among the Indians. One of those he met was a British trader to the Seminoles, whom he described as "a stout genteel well-bred man, active, and of a heroic and amiable disposition, and by his industry, honesty, and engaging manners, had gained the affections of the Indians, and soon made a little fortune by traffic with the Siminoles." The trader, however, had fallen in love with a "little charmer," a young Seminole woman who, according to Bartram, "possesses every perfection in her person to render a man happy" and "they were married in the Indian manner," that is, without Christian rites. Native people in the Southeast normally wed with little ceremony, made no long-term commitments, and parted easily if either spouse became

1

dissatisfied. We know very little about the Native women who married European men, but the common conjecture has been that these women lived in their husbands' houses, served their needs, and adapted to their culture. The trader whom Bartram encountered, however, confronted a different reality: "Innocence, modesty, and love, appear to a stranger in [her] every action and movement; and these powerful graces she has so artfully played upon her beguiled and vanquished lover, and unhappy slave, as to have already drained him of all his possessions, which she dishonestly distributes amongst her savage relations." Her husband threatened to shoot her and kill himself, but "he has not even resolution to leave her; but now endeavors to drown and forget his sorrows, in deep draughts of brandy."[1] The trader apparently could not accept the Native practice that gave control of households and their goods to women, and he could not force his wife to conform to his sense of propriety. His experience suggests that southern Indians expected foreigners to live by Native rules, even if that meant surrendering to wives and in-laws most of one's possessions. Native nations enjoyed both political and cultural sovereignty in the eighteenth century, and they incorporated foreigners into their societies on their own terms and for their own purposes. Most of those who stayed learned to live as well as to marry "in the Indian manner."

Foreigners abounded in Indian country in the eighteenth century. The Frenchman Antoine Bonnefoy, whom a Cherokee war party captured in 1741, discovered remarkable diversity among the residents of Tellico in what is today east Tennessee. Despite the town's location far from any European settlement, residents included three English traders and two of their servants, two Frenchmen, a German, and an African American couple who previously had been slaves of "the widow Saussier," but whose current status was unclear.[2] Other southern Indian towns mirrored the ethnic mélange at Tellico. Indian country beckoned traders, colonial

officials, squatters, criminals, and escaped slaves, and Indian warriors took captives from frontier settlements and parties traveling
through their territory. Some, like Bonnefoy, stayed only a few
months, whereas others remained permanently. However long foreigners stayed in Indian country, they became a part of an increasingly cosmopolitan Native world in which tribes incorporated not
only a new material culture of woven fabric and metal tools and
new ideas about economic exchange and political power, but also
new people.

A variety of circumstances landed foreigners in Native commu
nities. Rutel was a Breton sailor who got lost from La Salle's expedition down the Mississippi in 1682. The Caddos found him in
what is now Arkansas and adopted him. When Rutel "frightened
and routed the enemies of the Caddoes by using his rifle, which
was still an unknown weapon among them at that time," they accepted him as a warrior and permitted him to marry among them.[3]
John Pitchlynn was raised by the Choctaws after his father, a British
official, became ill and died while traveling through their country.[4] Pitchlynn ultimately married two Choctaw women, fathered
several Choctaw children (including a future chief), and became a
trusted interpreter in Choctaw dealings with the United States.[5]

A number of European colonists made conscious decisions to
live with the Indians.[6] Some saw Native peoples as a cultural *ta-
bula rasa* and sought to implement their own political and utopian
schemes among them. William Augustus Bowles, for example,
envisioned himself as the champion of Creek commercial and political independence, while Christian Gottlieb Priber tried to establish among the Cherokees his "kingdom of paradise," a utopia
devoid of private property, monogamous marriage, and racial distinctions.[7] Both entered the historical record because the English
regarded them as subversive, but far more common were the hundreds of people, many of whom remain nameless, who simply

sought opportunity and freedom on the other side of the colonial frontier. Nathaniel Folsom, for example, was a teenager traveling to Mississippi with his family when he and his father had a disagreement and he decided to remain in the Choctaw Nation.[8] He married two Choctaw women, and his sons came to play prominent roles in nineteenth-century Choctaw politics. Official business and the vagaries of empire brought other Europeans to Indian country. Traders and agents of England, France, and Spain were omnipresent, and when imperial fortunes shifted, many chose to remain in Native communities. During the American Revolution, many loyalists in the South took refuge with the Indians, who generally maintained neutrality or sided with Britain. Even after the war ended, the loyalists stayed.

African Americans entered Indian country of their own volition as readily as did Europeans. Slaves fled southern plantations, and free African Americans sought both opportunity on the frontier and reprieve from increasingly repressive colonial societies. Some African Americans apparently became incorporated into Indian society and enjoyed prominent positions, especially in the Creek and Seminole nations. Ninnywageechee, described as a "half breed negro," was a trader whose substantial debt to the British trading firm, Panton Leslie, suggests high status because only well-placed individuals and astute businessmen received credit. Philatouche, another African Creek, allied with William Augustus Bowles and received a commission from Lord Dunmore.[9] The Creeks accepted Africans into their society because traditionally Creeks had no concept of race. Kinship, not physical features, distinguished one Creek individual from another, and the Africans whom Indians incorporated had matrilineal ties to Creek clans through birth or adoption.

Even after the Creeks and other southern Indians began to adopt the racial attitudes of Europeans, kinship often overrode racial con-

siderations. In the 1770s, for example, a white trader by the name of
Samuel Bend presented an African American slave woman, whom
he had purchased in South Carolina, to the Cherokee Deer clan,
his in-laws, as a replacement for his wife, whom he had killed. The
clan, with the approbation of the council at Chota, accepted his offer and adopted the woman, who changed her name from Molly to
Chickaw. She ultimately married a Cherokee man and bore two
sons who enjoyed all the privileges of Cherokee citizenship. In
1833, when a white woman claimed Molly/Chickaw and one of her
sons as slaves whom she had inherited from her father, the Council
determined "to resist this oppression and illegal wrong attempted
to be practiced on our Brother and Sister . . . in carrying into slavery Two of whom have been and considered native Cherokee."[10]
The members of the council declared Molly/Chickaw and her son
free. Most African Americans were not so fortunate, particularly
as racial slavery became entrenched among southern Indians in
the nineteenth century. Changing racial views led Native people
increasingly to distance themselves from African Americans and
to regard foreigners with black skins to be more suitable as slaves
than as adoptive relatives.[11]

While some African Americans, like Molly, found refuge in Indian country, most became merely another commodity in the Indians' expanding commercial economies.[12] Colonists paid bounties
to Native people for the return of their escaped slaves, a measure
that served two purposes. First, masters recovered their slaves, and
second, they fostered enmity between Indians and Africans, who
might otherwise have found common ground on which to rebel
against colonial oppression.[13] Rewards made runaway slaves commodities rather than potential allies. In the late eighteenth century,
for example, Cherokee warriors discovered two African American
men who had escaped from their masters, descended the Holston

River into uninhabited Cherokee country in east Tennessee, and carved a farm out of the dense forest. Unsympathetic to their situation, the warriors returned the fugitives to their masters.[14]

Warriors quickly learned that the sale of African American slaves whom they had captured brought a better return than their ransom. Southern Indians had long sold war captives from enemy tribes to colonists, who enslaved them, but the extirpation of small tribes and the dangers posed by wars among more powerful foes led to a decline in the demand for Indian slaves. The seizure of African American slaves in one locale and their sale in another promised far greater financial returns at substantially less risk. Furthermore, southern Indians often used these captives as an investment, holding them until they needed goods and then selling them to whites or to other Indians. Eighteenth-century observers often commented on the Indians' failure to exact labor from their slaves. United States Indian Agent Benjamin Hawkins, for example, complained that Efau Hadjo, one of the principal Creek headmen, had five slaves who were "of little use to him."[15] In fact, their labor was of little use to him, but their market value was of great benefit.

As Indians recognized slaves' financial worth, colonial officials encountered considerable difficulty in securing their return to their original masters. In 1772 British official David Taitt managed to retrieve an African American slave taken by Creeks in a frontier raid that claimed the life of the slave woman's husband and daughter, but he could not regain possession of her son, who had changed hands at least three times since his capture.[16] The illicit market in African American slaves meant that no person of color was safe on the frontier. Hawkins, for example, had to negotiate the release and return of Polly Russell, a free woman whom Creek warriors had kidnapped and sold into slavery.[17] By the end of the eighteenth century, some warriors raided the frontier solely to obtain African Americans for the illicit slave trade.

Although the commercial traffic in slaves was a new development, Indian warfare traditionally had included the seizure of captives. Many of those captives, both African American and white, ultimately died, some as a result of torture. Compatriots ransomed others, but Indians attempted to convert those who remained with them into Indians. The Creeks, for example, killed one of three white women they captured in 1792 in the Cumberland settlement of central Tennessee because she had been wounded in the attack and could not keep up with the retreating war party. They took the two other women to their town Kialegee, however, and tried to incorporate them into Creek society by putting them to work in the fields with Creek women. The white women resented this treatment, which they interpreted as slavery, and the younger one wept so bitterly that her captors permitted her to pound corn instead of cultivate it. When she proved no better at this task, the Creeks agreed to return her to her people in exchange for eight hundred pounds of dressed deerskins. The older woman remained in the fields, and the Creeks sought to enhance her stamina by scratching her with gar teeth, a ritual they administered to ball players and even their own children in order to give them strength, but their captive viewed the treatment as torture. After two years in captivity, she too was redeemed. From the perspective of these two women, the Creeks had been cruel taskmasters, but from the Creek perspective, they simply had tried to turn these women into Creeks.[18]

Southern Indians formally incorporated many foreigners into their society through adoption. Antoine Bonnefoy, whom Cherokees captured in 1741 and took to Tellico, was adopted. While on their way to Tellico, one warrior purchased Bonnefoy from a fellow member of the war party, and upon their arrival, he formally presented the Frenchman to his family, probably as the replacement for a dead brother. The town council conferred and presumably assented, and the family conducted an adoption ceremony that included feasting, singing, painting Bonnefoy's body, and burying a lock of his hair. The Cherokees never treated Bonnefoy like a captive: he lived as they did, and he was free to come and go as he pleased.[19]

As an adopted male captive, Bonnefoy was something of an anomaly. Normally warriors killed men on the battlefield or brought them back to their town for torture and execution. Women and children were far more likely candidates for adoption.[20] Most southern tribes had many members who had not been born to them, although the Cherokees apparently carried adoption to the extreme. When a Mohawk, Major John Norton, toured the Cherokee Nation in the early nineteenth century, he discovered a number of his own people as well as Europeans and Natives of other nations living there as adopted Cherokees. Because of "their universal custom of adopting in their own Nation the captive females and youths they had taken from hostile tribes," the Cherokees, he observed, had "less regularity" in their appearance than other Indians.[21]

Most of the European women who lived among the southern Indians in the eighteenth and early nineteenth centuries were adopted captives. Many had lived with their Indian families since childhood, married Indian men, and given birth to children who inherited a secure place within Indian society as well as, perhaps, their fathers' dark skin and hair. A few of these women made what must have been wrenching decisions to return to white society. A white woman whom Shoe Boots, a distinguished Cherokee leader, had captured as a child and married when she reached adulthood, for example, finally yielded to the repeated demands of her family in Kentucky that she return to them. Taking their three children with her, she left the old warrior and the people with whom she had lived for most of her life and embarked on what proved to be a disappointing life among whites.[22]

Most women, however, made a different choice.[23] In 1772 British official David Taitt failed to recover a captive white woman whom Creek chiefs had agreed to surrender because she had "run off with an Indian who is her husband, so that they Could not find her."[24] Hlikukhto, or Hummingbird, a Chickasaw warrior, reportedly captured a five-year-old French girl named Nancy. As soon as she reached maturity, he married her, and they had a large family. One white observer reported that at age ninety-one "she still retained her European features, . . . but in every other respect was a Chickasaw."[25] Interestingly, the white observer first noted her appearance, something that mattered little to the Chickasaws. In the 1790s Hannah Hales, whom Creek warriors had captured in Georgia, rebuffed her white relatives who entreated her to come home when hostilities ended. Adopted by the Creeks, Hales "possesse[d] the rights of a Creek woman." Free to use unoccupied land, she had managed to acquire horses, cattle, and hogs, as well as an African American slave, all of which, according to Creek law, she held separately from her husband.[26] The Creeks had succeeded in making her one of their own.

For southern Indians, human beings fell into two camps—relatives, who belonged within the community, and enemies, who did not. If a person had no ties of kinship to the community and no position within it, Native southerners regarded that person as an enemy, and enemies had no rights, not even the right to live.[27] Only the formal incorporation of an individual into the community through ritual transformed an enemy into a relative. From the Native perspective, Bonnefoy and Hales, like other Europeans who were adopted, literally became Cherokee and Creek respectively because they became relatives, and the Indians expected them to remain permanently in the community with their new kin. Circumstances, however, sometimes demanded that a tribe convert enemies into relatives in order to open the door to peaceful relations between two peoples. In 1785–86 at the first meeting between

Choctaws and commissioners of the new United States in upcoun-
try South Carolina, for example, Choctaw women embraced the
American commissioners one by one, presumably conveying on
them a temporary, or fictive, kin tie that made the negotiation of
the Hopewell Treaty possible.[28]

Southern Indians regarded their own communities as safe and
orderly, but beyond these communities lay chaos. They were leery
of anything that emerged from the chaos, and they sought to impose on it the order that they carefully maintained within their communities by integrating outsiders in a number of ways. Ceremony
marked the entrance of foreigners into a Native community. Mingo
Chito, a Choctaw chief, for example, would not permit a French
diplomat to walk across the square ground that lay at the heart of
his town until he had performed the requisite rituals. An "honored
man" carried the startled envoy on his back while others shaded
him from the sun, which the Choctaws regarded as a deity whose
light they did not want to shine on the profane in the sacred space
of their square ground.[29] The Creeks ushered strangers into their
town house or square ground, sang sacred songs, and offered them
conch shells filled with the spiritually purifying black drink, a tea
made of yaupon holly.[30] Cherokees placed South Carolina Indian
Commissioner George Chicken "in a Great Chair in the most Publick Place in Town" and fanned him with eagle feathers. After the
chief spoke, warriors fired a volley over Chicken's head and led
him to the house of the resident trader, where they smoked their
ceremonial pipes with him.[31] Sometimes less formal rites clarified
a person's presence and indicated his acceptance. The experience
of William Bartram in the Seminole town of Cuscowilla can be understood in this context. Upon his arrival, young men and women
conducted the naturalist to the chief's house, where the headman
and council invited him to smoke with them and eat sofkey, the
Creek version of grits, which played a ceremonial as well as a culi-

nary role. Bartram explained his presence in their territory, and the chief, convinced that he was harmless, gave him a Creek name, Puc Puggy or Flower Hunter.[32] Through ritual, Indians transformed people like Bartram, who could have been disruptive, into harmonious members of the community.

More than likely, European traders, agents, and emissaries became adoptive or fictive kin to the people with whom they interacted, and they received Indian titles or names that indicated their acceptance as members of the community. In 1765, at a meeting between Choctaw and British officials, the Choctaws conferred the title Chactimataha Chito, "Great Supporter of the Choctaw People," on John Stuart, the Indian Superintendent South of the Ohio, and Fanimingo Mattaha, "Supporter of the Calumet Chief," on British Lieutenant Colonel David Wedderburne. Other participants received titles that made them "Supporters" of the two major ethnic groups in the Choctaw Nation—Imoklasha Mattaha and Inhulahta Mattaha.[33] At the congress of Pensacola in 1771, the Creeks gave the name Alibama Mico to Stuart because the Alibamas were "great in war and in peace and solicitous for the good of all the tribes." Florida governor Peter Chester received the title Apalachicola Mico, the highest title they could convey, because, they explained, the Apalachicolas were the "original proprietors" of the land. General Frederick Haldiman became Cusseta Mico since the Cussetas "were always noted warriors."[34] The Creeks called long-time United States Agent Benjamin Hawkins "most beloved man," the same title they used for Alexander McGillivray, a Creek headman who tried to unite them into a centralized nation in the late eighteenth century.[35] Among the Cherokees, British Superintendent John Stuart, who was formally adopted, bore a Cherokee name that is translated "Bushyhead"; his Indian descendants still use the anglicized word as their surname.[36]

Native people did not require foreign diplomats, traders, and travelers to fully understand or obey all the rigid kin rules of respect, avoidance, joking, and hospitality, but they did expect reciprocity, the fundamental principle on which relationships within Native communities rested. Foreigners who were successful in their relations with Indians understood this. General James Oglethorpe of Georgia, for example, publicly offered presents to Indian delegations on the square in Savannah. The observer who recorded these proceedings couched his description in terms of reciprocity: by giving "the Indians the Presents he had Caused to be brought for them," Oglethorpe "Establish[ed] that Peace with them which has since been so Beneficial to the English" and "settled the Trade between the Indians and the Traders."[37] The Indians received gifts; the English received peace and trade. Reciprocity with real and fictive kin also existed on a more informal and personal level. John Lawson reported that North Carolina Indians permitted English traders "to take out of their Houses what they need in their absence, in Lieu whereof they most commonly leave some small Gratuity of Tobacco, Paint, Beads, &c."[38]

Related to the principle of reciprocity was the practice of redistribution. Europeans who entered Indian country first encountered this practice in the form of hospitality, which naturalist Bernard Romans believed "they carry to excess; a savage will share his last ounce of meat with a visitant stranger."[39] Chiefs received surplus food from their own people and gifts from outsiders, and then they redistributed the goods in the form of feasts, rewards, hospitality, and subsidies for the poor. Creek chiefs tried to educate Hawkins about the practice when they invited him to visit the town of Tuckabatchee following the completion of a public works project: "It is usual on such occasions for all connected with our town by marriage or otherwise to attend or send in some acknowledgement of provisions or something if it be but a chalk [quarter of a dollar] a piece."[40] Colonial officials, particularly the English, resented their role in redistribution, which was primarily as purveyors of gifts, and after the Revolution, the United States tried to bring the practice to a halt.[41] Some Europeans also regarded the role of chiefs in acquiring goods from their own people as "cheating" and "black and crooked."[42] Bartram pointed out, however, that the houses of chiefs generally were indistinguishable from those of other villagers, and they and their families hunted and farmed just like everyone else. The only advantage chiefs had was "the disposal of the Corn & Fruits in the publick or National Granary," and that was for the good of all.[43] When they visited Native towns, Europeans became the beneficiaries of this Native largesse. In 1725, for example, the chief at Okfuskey placed food before a colonial emissary and, conscious of the principle of reciprocity as well as hospitality, told him: "I am Glad to see you here In my Town But I am Sory that I Cannot Entertain you With Such as I am Entertained When I go Down to your Great Town; But I hope you will Except [*sic*] of Such as I have and you are very Welcom to it."[44]

During the American Revolution, many British soldiers and loyalists took refuge in Indian country, but before then most non-Indians who lived for extended periods of time in Native communities were traders. One of the most important commercial activities in the colonial South was the Indian trade. Southern forests teemed with deer, which Native hunters killed for their skins. Although Indians also sold war captives from other tribes as slaves and marketed a variety of commodities ranging from beeswax to baskets, deerskins were the staple of the trade. Merchants in Charleston, Savannah, Augusta, and Pensacola outfitted traders with a variety of European goods. Human porters and later packhorses carried loads of knives, hatchets, kettles, scissors, hoe blades, eyeglasses, mirrors, beads, blankets and other fabrics, guns and ammunition, and rum from colonial towns to Native ones. Traders at first set up shop only during hunting season. Year-round residency, however,

proved a far more satisfactory way of doing business, and traders
soon established permanent businesses in specific towns. Sales on
credit throughout the year bound a hunter to the trader who advanced him goods, but the trader soon became caught in a social
as well as an economic web.[45]

Headmen tried to ensure that traders conformed to Native culture. Before the British deregulated the trade in 1763, chiefs granted
permission for foreigners to trade in specific towns and closely
monitored the activities of traders. After the Proclamation of 1763
suspended colonial regulation, unscrupulous white men flooded Indian country, conducted business in hunting grounds away from
the watchful eyes of chiefs, and flaunted the chiefs' authority even
when they were in the villages. The Creek Captain of Hocktawella
complained to colonial official David Taitt that three traders had
located in his town, which had only seventy hunters: "When the
last trader came there which is about two months ago the head
men advised him not to open his goods but go somewhere else, but
their advise [sic] was to no good purpose."[46] Without clear authority
to halt the influx of traders, colonial governments could offer the
chiefs little relief.

Even under these adverse conditions, however, chiefs asserted
their authority. Just as chiefs regulated the trade by admitting traders to towns, soliciting gifts from them, and demanding compliance
with Native customs, they also controlled the access of foreigners to women. In the first decade of the eighteenth century, John
Lawson discovered that when a foreigner approached a young Indian woman about a sexual liaison, she informed her parents, who
notified the chief. The chief and his advisors then "debate[d] the
Matter amongst themselves with all the Sobriety and Seriousness
imaginable, every one of the Girls' relations arguing the Advantage or Detriment that may ensue a Night's Encounter; all which is
done with as much Steadiness and Reality, as if it was the greatest

Concern in the World, and not so much as one Person shall be seen to smile, as long as the debate holds, making no Difference betwixt an Agreement of this Nature, and a Bargain of any other."[47] This process differed dramatically from the courtship of a woman by a member of her own tribe: "If it be an *Indian* of their own Town or Neighbourhood, that wants a Mistress, he comes to none but the Girl, who receives what she thinks fit to ask him, and so lies all Night with him, without the Consent of her Parents."[48] Among her own people, a woman enjoyed considerable sexual autonomy; sex with a foreigner was an entirely different matter that involved the welfare of the entire community and the power and prestige of the chief.

Virtually all the Europeans who traded in Indian country for any length of time took Native wives and became known as "Indian Countrymen." As early as the first decade of the eighteenth century, John Lawson noted that "The *English* traders are seldom without an *Indian* Female for his Bed-fellow."[49] These traders, however, had more compelling reasons than sex to develop relationships with Native women. Europeans needed wives in Indian country because a man without a wife did not eat except at great expense and with constant uncertainty. Native people divided labor according to gender, with women farming and men hunting, and awarded each the product of his or her labor.[50] Women also processed both game and vegetables to make them edible: they soaked and pounded dry corn, dressed and butchered deer, carried water and firewood, and prepared all of a family's food. Women normally were very hospitable to strangers and freely offered them food, but marriage provided a more secure food supply since familial obligations, including those of wives to husbands, often overrode political and economic concerns.

Chiefs rigidly controlled the agricultural productivity of traders and prevented them from becoming too independent by limiting livestock and land use. Taitt wrote Superintendent John Stuart that Creek chiefs had "agreed to let what Cattle the Traders have in this nation Remain alive, but no more to be brought amongst them and no plantations to be made by the traders."[51] Unable to farm or keep herds, traders and other foreigners had to depend on Indians for food, and that meant depending on women, who controlled the food supply. In the 1750s the garrison at Fort Loudoun in east Tennessee had to hire a Cherokee woman as purchasing agent in order to obtain sufficient provisions, and when Agent Hawkins visited the Cherokees at the end of the eighteenth century, he "went over to John Candy's house and purchased from his wife some corn, potatoes and fodder."[52]

The only way for a foreign man to obtain land was to marry a Native woman and thereby socially bind himself to the community. Agricultural land and homesteads vested in matrilineal and matrilocal households, so a man without a wife had no access to cleared fields and no right to establish a domicile. A matrilineage was a multigenerational extended household whose permanent residents were related women (sisters, mothers and aunts, and their children), unmarried male relatives, and the women's husbands. According to Hawkins, in these households the husband was "a tenant at will."[53] Although matrilineages might have marked off individual plots within the fields, labor was communal, and the whole town usually joined the women in the fall harvest of corn, beans, and squash. Forests or abandoned "old fields" surrounded the cultivated fields, and according to Bartram's description of the Creeks, "every individual citizen of the Confederacy have the same equal right to hunt and range where he pleases, in the forests and unoccupied lands, and to range stocks of cattle, horses, &ca." A citizen, that is a person who belonged to a Creek matrilineage, had the right to "clear, settle & plant as much land as he pleases and wherever he will, within the boundaries of his tribe [or town]," but there were few "Farms or Private plantations, out of sight of the town."[54]

When Hawkins arrived among the Creeks as United States
Agent in the 1790s, trader Daniel McGillivray told him that "when
he applied to the indians for permission to settle out of town they
brought him to this spot, marked the front on the river and permitted him to call all his that he could clear and cultivate." The
headmen carefully controlled where McGillivray lived, but what
entitled him to use the land was the fact that "he has a Creek woman
and a son 6 years old."[55] The other southern tribes also limited
access to land and its resources, including forage for livestock. According to Bartram, a trader he encountered "was indulged to keep
a stock of cattle" only by virtue of his "being married to a Cherokee
woman of family."[56]

Indian women exercised considerable power when it came to
land use, and the wives of traders often used that power to the advantage of their husbands. Trader Richard Bailey moved to Tensaw,
a new town on the Creek frontier, after the headmen at Autossee,
where he had been living with his wife and conducting his business, complained about his livestock destroying their crops. As a
result, Autossee was three years without a resident trader, and the
resulting hardship prompted the headmen to encourage Bailey and
his family to return. Bailey's Creek wife drove a hard bargain: "She
would not unless their stock could be secure, and it should be left
to Mr. Bailey to choose his place of residence near the town." The
headmen agreed, the Baileys returned, and the Creeks adhered to
the agreement "with some little murmuring." Although the desire
for trade forced a reconsideration of the Baileys' exile, the rights of
his wife as a Creek woman enabled him to obtain concessions that
made his residence in Autossee tenable.[57]

Mrs. Bailey clearly was a woman to be reckoned with. By the
time Agent Hawkins encountered the family in the 1790s, Richard
Bailey had been in Creek country for forty years, and he and his
wife were parents to grown children. The Baileys owned seven
slaves as well as 200 head of cattle, 120 horses, and 150 hogs. Mrs.

Bailey, according to Hawkins, "governs her black people and shows much attention to the stock about the plantation." Two slave women assisted her with domestic chores, but she reportedly did "much of it with her own hands," including churning butter. In addition, "she sometimes beats the meal for bread, sifts it and bakes it herself." Although she did not permit other Creeks to take advantage of her prosperity, she was "agreeable and jocose in conversation, [and] kind to everybody." She carefully conformed to the Creek hospitality ethic, and when Hawkins visited the Baileys, she served a dinner of bread and butter, "a relish of some kind of meat," "fowls and pork with rice," and coffee and tea. Hawkins reported that Mrs. Bailey also "share[d] in all the toils of her husband when there was a necessity for it. She attended the pack horses to market, [and] swam rivers to facilitate the transportation of their goods."[58]

Some traders' wives participated in their husbands' businesses in a less scrupulous way, one that involved the taste many Native men had acquired for alcohol. A trader normally supplied hunters with goods ranging from fabric and metal tools to guns and ammunition. Traders also sold rum, usually well watered but alcoholic enough to produce drunkenness. Sensible traders realized that they needed to provide hunters with more than simply alcohol if they were to sustain commerce, but the avaricious, fly-by-night traders who flocked to Indian country after 1763 were more interested in the fast buck than the long haul. One such man, about whom David Taitt complained in 1772, met a hunting party as it returned to town and purchased all the skins with rum, depriving other traders of a share in the hunt and the Indians of necessities. Even when this trader sold them utilitarian goods, he sent his wife to exchange rum for the merchandise so that he could outfit the hunters a second time on credit, which bound them to him, and each exchange enhanced his profit.[59] Some women engaged in the rum trade in less orthodox ways. Bartram observed women who feigned drinking with men but spit their rum into an empty bottle, "and when the comic farce is over, the wench retails this precious cordial to them at her own price."[60]

The most important role that most wives played in commerce, however, was that of translator and language instructor. "Besides the Satisfaction of a She-Bed-Fellow," according to John Lawson, traders married Indian women to "learn the *Indian* Tongue."[61] The large southern tribes, except for the Cherokees whose language falls into the Iroquoian family, spoke Muskogean languages, but most were not mutually intelligible. Traders frequently employed a *lingua franca,* called Mobilian, but its limited vocabulary and simplified grammar made Mobilian inadequate for everyday life.[62] Fluency in a Native language not only made a trader's life more enjoyable, but it also enabled him to interact directly with his customers; follow local politics, which often had a considerable impact on his livelihood and sometimes his life; and act as translator for other foreigners, a role that enhanced his status in the community. With the help of their wives and in-laws, most traders became quite fluent. Trader James Adair claimed that James Logan Colbert, who married three Chickasaw women in the early eighteenth century, spoke "their language with even more propriety" than he spoke English.[63]

A trader's wife also educated him in "the Affairs and Customs of the Country" and prevented him from making a *faux pas* that could jeopardize his financial success and personal safety.[64] For example, learning to extinguish fire, the earthly representative of the sun and the upper world, with soil, the mediating substance of this world, and not water, which led to the underworld, reassured a trader's customers and neighbors that he was not violating the carefully ordered harmony of the cosmos. Abstaining from the consumption of green corn until after the appropriate ceremony acknowledged his respect for Native beliefs and contributed to his acceptance in the community.[65] Traders probably did not intend to become culturally Indian, but over the years most adopted various cultural practices that their wives taught them. Benjamin Hawkins, for example, attributed the good health of trader Richard Bailey's family to "a custom continued by Mrs. Bailey, she and her family every morning winter or summer bathe in cold water."[66] Southern Indians practiced "going to water," as they called it, not as a matter of personal hygiene but as spiritual cleansing, and even if Mr. Bailey, like Hawkins, misinterpreted its meaning, he still performed the culturally appropriate ablution.

Other Europeans clearly adopted certain Native beliefs. Two white traders, whom their colleague James Adair ridiculed, each sewed a deer foot in his hunting pouch to bring good luck. Much to the dismay of another trader, Adair killed a rattlesnake whose teeth the man had just removed in an Indian ritual. Wearing nothing except "his Indian breeches and maccaseenes," the trader had "laid it down tenderly at some distance" as Native practice required, and he was convinced that Adair's lethal blow would bring them both misfortune.[67] Other traders believed in witches and "report[ed] very incredible and shocking stories." When they camped at the abandoned Creek town of Ocmulgee, some traders claimed to hear singing as the shades of former residents went to water and returned to the town house, but Adair scoffed. When he camped at the site, "all hath been silent."[68] Although Adair, who had Cherokee and Chickasaw wives, disparaged these practices and beliefs, he apparently became convinced of the existence of the Uktena, a mythical serpent the Cherokees believed lived in the high mountains of their country.[69]

Connections to their wives' kin groups further integrated Europeans into Indian life. Clans organized Native societies, and only birth or adoption into a clan conveyed tribal citizenship.[70] Clan members lived dispersed throughout tribal territory, and clans

served to unify tribes even in the absence of centralized government. Being matrilineal, southern Indians inherited their clans from
their mothers, and marriage did not alter clan affiliation. Indian
clans may have adopted some traders and thereby extended to
them full tribal citizenship. Among the Cherokees, for example,
several intermarried white men had Cherokee names, which may
have signaled their status as adoptive or fictive kin. John Walker and
John McDonald, for example, were Sequanyoho (or Sisuaniyoho)
and Thoghweliska, respectively.[71]

Most intermarried whites, however, seem to have participated
in the kinship system primarily as the husbands of Native women.
Thomas Nairne observed: "It is the easyest thing in the world, for
an English Traveller to procure kindred among the Indians, It's but
taking a mistress of such a name, and he has at once relations in
each Village, from Charles Town to the Missisipi, and if in travelling
he aquants them with what fameily he is incorporated into, those of
that name treat, and wait on him as their kinsman. There are some
of our Countryman of such prudence and forecast, that in case one
family should fail them, take care to make themselves akin to sever-
all."[72] Marriage did not provide clan ties, as only birth and adoption
did that, but marriage to a clan member established rules of deco-
rum and assured the trader of hospitality and friendship throughout the nation. Other members of the community knew how to
behave toward the husband of a particular clan member. Furthermore, marriage engendered customer loyalty among a trader's in-
laws, and the failure to marry an Indian woman often doomed a
white man's business. Lawson remarked, "such a man gets a great
Trade with the Savages; for when a Person that lives amongst them,
is reserv'd from the Conversation of their Women, 'tis impossible
for him ever to accomplish his Designs amongst that People."[73]

A Native wife and in-laws provided a trader with some security
in Indian country. The law of blood, by which southern Indians

regulated behavior through vengeance, did not extend to white traders unless they had been adopted. Without clan kin, traders had no one to guarantee their safety, which colonial wars often jeopardized, but in the words of trader James Adair, he and his intermarried colleagues "stood secure in the affection of . . . savage brethren." During the French and Indian War "in the day-time, they kept in the most unfrequented places, and usually returned at night to their friend's house." "Friend," as Adair used the word, referred to wives. The Creek wife of one trader saved her husband's life when two warriors allied to the French came to their house to kill him. As one reached for an axe that was lying on the floor of the storehouse, she seized it and shouted, "husband fight strong, and run off, as becomes a good warrior." The trader did as commanded and fled to safety on the opposite side of the river. According to Adair, "the woman, as a trusted friend, drove them off, with the utmost despight, —her family was her protection."[74] In the same conflict, the wives of the British soldiers who garrisoned Fort Loudoun, in what is today east Tennessee, defied the war chief who had the fort under siege and, reported Lieutenant Henry Timberlake, "brought them a daily supply of provisions." The war chief threatened to kill the women if they did not desist, "But they laughing at his threats, boldly told him, they would succor their husbands every day, and were sure, that, if he killed them, their relations would make his death atone for theirs." The war chief backed down.[75] Indian wives also enabled officials to save the lives of colonists. In the Natchez Revolt of 1729, a Natchez woman tipped off her lover, the French commander, about the planned attack, thereby reducing casualties, and in 1792 Leonard Shaw, United States agent to the Cherokees, learned about a plot to attack the Holston settlements from his Cherokee wife in time to warn the residents to flee to safety.[76]

While traders and others who intermarried easily perceived the

advantages of taking an Indian wife, they did not so quickly recognize the benefits that accrued to wives and their families from
marriage to a foreigner. Many, such as the British trader who married the "little charmer," learned the hard way. Bartram assured
his readers that this woman's father disapproved of her "dishonest
and cruel conduct" and that her people "condemned and detested"
her character, but his account reveals that her relatives shared in
the goods purloined from her husband.[77] The "little charmer" and
her kin no doubt believed that they had a claim on these goods
because they were in the trader's house, which, in a matrilocal society, where husbands lived with wives, was actually her house.
The goods she distributed from the house were also hers, and her
generosity to kin was socially sanctioned behavior. Bartram may
have been horrified and the trader distraught, but when the "little charmer's" father and others criticized her, they probably were
only politely agreeing with guests.

Benjamin Hawkins encountered similar problems at the United
States agency. Hawkins initially had favored intermarriage and considered taking an Indian wife himself, but he soon concluded "that
a white man marrying an Indian woman of the Creek Nation so
far from bettering his condition becomes a slave to her family."[78]
When the blacksmith at the agency took a Creek wife, the result
was disastrous: "The wife and [her] family first took direction of
the provisions, then the house and pay and finally the absolute government of every thing at the agency whether connected with the
Smith or not." Ultimately, the smith and his wife separated, but the
experience prompted Hawkins to forbid employees of the agency
to marry Creek women and to prohibit "all amorous intercourse
between red and white people at the agency."[79]

Native people recognized that intermarriage brought material
advantages to the families to whom traders, soldiers, agents, and
other officials connected themselves. Consequently, politically

powerful families tried to monopolize intermarriage, and Europeans normally married into the families of chiefs or clans that customarily produced chiefs. Clans are difficult to discern because most European observers were unaware of or uninterested in them, but evidence does reveal that the indomitable Mrs. Bailey was a member of the Wind clan, arguably the most prestigious of Creek clans.[80] Charleston trader Edward Griffin married a sister of the Creek "Emperor" Brims, probably of the Wind clan, and fathered the woman who became known to eighteenth-century Georgians as Mary Musgrove.[81] Trader Bryan Ward married Nancy, niece of the Cherokees' most prominent eighteenth-century chief Attakullakulla, and Brigadier General Joseph Martin, North Carolina agent to the Cherokees, married their daughter.[82] Leonard Shaw, agent to the Cherokees in the 1790s, married "a chief's daughter," and a trader and interpreter named Watts married a sister of Old Tassel, the principal chief of the Upper Cherokees.[83] The "little charmer" who reduced her trader husband to penury was the daughter of a Seminole chief named White Captain.[84] Among the Choctaws, Charles Juzan, a Frenchman, married a niece of Pushmataha, a prominent chief, and Major John Pitchlynn "took a wife when a young man from a powerful family of natives."[85] Nathaniel Folsom, in the Native tradition of sororal polygamy, married two sisters, nieces of Choctaw chief Miko Pushkush. According to nineteenth-century historian Horatio Cushman, Folsom's wives "descended from a long ancient line of chiefs, and belonged to the ancient Iksa Hattakiholihta, one of the two great families."[86] Less prestigious marriages also probably took place, but virtually all of the next generation of Native leaders who had white fathers and whose maternal lineage is known descended from politically and socially powerful Native families.

When powerful families allied themselves to traders and other foreigners through marriage they did not simply seek financial gain.

Intermarriage was, on one level, another way that Native people ritually incorporated foreigners; they attempted to dispel the chaos from which they had come, impose order on them, and harness the spiritual power, represented by new ideas and goods, that foreigners coming from the chaos presumably possessed. Marriage was an effective way to accomplish these goals because it brought the foreigner under the social control of Native people and made possible the Native acquisition of any inherent spiritual power through close association and inheritance. They obtained that power, in part, when Native women bore children by white men because they considered the children to be Indian, not white or "mixed blood." Lawson described Native people as "esteeming a white Man's Child much above one of their getting," a view that he believed indicated their recognition of European superiority. In reality, Native people probably saw themselves as appropriating—and extinguishing—whiteness by transforming a white man's offspring into Indians.[87] Their ability to incorporate foreigners and gain access to their power suggested to them their own preeminence. Furthermore, they did not regard women who married foreigners as subservient or a form of tribute; they were autonomous individuals who, like all good citizens, placed community and family first. Marriage to a foreigner, like the possession of exotic goods, may well have been a mark of high status, because the elite seem to have tried to monopolize such unions.

Europeans, on the other hand, brought with them assumptions about race, culture, and gender that shaped their attitudes toward Native women and intermarriage. They regarded their own culture as superior to that of the Indians, and they saw their own treatment of women as evidence for that superiority. Hawkins haughtily told a Creek woman who tried to negotiate his marriage to her daughter, "We make companions of our women, the Indians make slaves of theirs."[88] In reality, Europeans viewed Indians as inferior to themselves and women as inferior to men. Hawkins commended Robert Grierson, a Scot trader, who "governs them [his Creek wife and children] as Indians," that is, inferiors, "and makes them and his whole family respect him."[89] Europeans also condoned the corporal punishment of wives as a means to physically enforce male superiority. On the other hand, Native southerners hit neither children nor spouses, and Indian families normally lived in egalitarian harmony. Bartram observed, "I have been weeks and months amongst them and in their towns, and never observed the least sign of contention or wrangling: never saw an instance of an Indian beating his wife, or even reproving her in anger. In this case they stand as examples of reproof to the most civilized nations."[90]

The one marital issue that had the potential to provoke violence was adultery, but men as well as women suffered in Native communities. While southern Indians permitted unmarried men and women considerable sexual freedom, and divorce and remarriage were common, all except the Cherokees severely punished adultery. The Creeks were particularly adamant, and sexual dalliances between married people could cost both men and women their ears, noses, and even lives.[91] Most European men had no clear conception of Native sexual rules, and they assumed that the liberties enjoyed by the unmarried and the ease with which Indians changed spouses meant that sexual intercourse with married women was acceptable.[92] Consequently, they often ran afoul of the law. William Bartram encountered a young trader who had the misfortune of having been discovered in a compromising situation with the wife of a Creek chief. The aggrieved husband and his friends went to the trader's house and stripped and beat him. Assuming that they intended to beat him to death, the trader feigned unconsciousness, but "the executioner drew out his knife with the intention of taking off his ears." At this point, the trader "sprang up, ran off, leaped the fence and had the good fortune to get into a dark swamp" where he eluded his attackers. Eventually he made it to the house of his wife's father (or perhaps uncle) who agreed to intercede for him, and ultimately the town council ruled "that he must loose his ears or forfeit all his goods."[93] We know nothing of the woman's fate, but Hawkins suggested that a Creek woman could ignore the strict laws against adultery if she was married to a white man: "If she commit whoredom it is no offense against a white husband and only makes him a subject of ridicule."[94]

Cherokee women had unparalleled sexual autonomy, which caused some traders who formed liaisons with them considerable heartache. James Adair reported that one particular Englishman, who had fallen in love with a Cherokee woman by the name of Dark-lathorn, devised a plan to secure her to him despite the fact "that marriages were commonly of short duration in that wanton female government." He engaged a minister to baptize her, instruct her in her "conjugal duty," and marry them in the church. Acting as translator in an interminably long session in which the rector revealed mysteries of Christianity to the impatient Cherokee woman, the groom disingenuously assured the cleric that Dark-lathorn fully comprehended the complex nature of the trinity. Elated over his first Native convert, the minister quickly entered her name into the church registry and married the couple. "Afterward to his great grief," according to Adair, "he was obliged on account of her adulteries, to erase her name from thence, and enter it anew in some of the crowded pages of female delinquencies."[95]

Despite the experience of Dark-lathorn's suitor, European men may have been more likely to end marriages than Native women. A Christian church did not sanction most unions; instead a couple married "in the Indian manner" with merely a familial agreement and exchange of gifts before cohabiting.[96] Consequently, European men did not feel bound to Native women and often returned to white wives in the colonies or the mother country. Since plural ves as well as frequent divorce and remarriage were common among southern Indians, women may not have expected any other behavior. John Lawson, however, "knew a *European* Man that had a Child or two by one of these *Indian* Women, and afterwards married a Christian, after which he came to pass away a Night with his *Indian* Mistress; but she[the Indian mistress] made Answer that she had then forgot she ever knew him, and that she never lay with another Woman's Husband, so fell a crying, and took up the Child she had by him, and went out of the Cabin (away from him) in great Disorder."[97]

Although some European men abandoned their Native families, others formed deep emotional attachments to their wives and children. James Adair adopted a decidedly affectionate tone as he recorded a recipe for preparing corn meal: "I have the pleasure of writing this by the side of a Chikkasah female, as great a princess as ever lived among the ancient Peruvians, or Mexicans, and she bids me be sure not to mark the paper wrong, after the manner of most of the traders; otherwise, it will spoil the making good bread, or hommony, and of course beget the ill-will of our white women."[98] Many white men lived for decades with their Indian families and died in their adopted nations. Trader Robert Grierson, for example, married a Creek woman, Sinnuggee, when he first went into Indian country in the 1770s, and by the time he met Hawkins twenty years later, he was a grandfather. He told Hawkins that he was "much attached to this country and means to spend his days here with his Indian family and connexions."[99] John McDonald, the British deputy superintendent, told John Norton that following the Revolution "his affection for his wife and children induced him to remain and share the fate of the Cherokees, to which nation his wife belonged." And a Canadian trader among the Cherokees remarked that he would return north "were it not for the love he bore his family."[100]

The political allegiances of white men who had married into Indian nations often rested with their wives' people. James Logan Colbert, a Scottish trader married to three Chickasaw women, organized defenses against the French in the mid–eighteenth century and led war parties against the Americans in the Revolution, including one that rebuffed an invasion by Virginians. Although his own ancestry may have predisposed him to fight for the Crown, he fought like and with Chickasaw warriors.[101] In 1776 Nathaniel Gist, who had lived in the Cherokee Nation with his Indian wife for twenty-five years and compiled a distinguished record of service as a liaison with whites, announced, "He himself had fought many a Day for the Country [but] now he should fight against it [meaning the United States]." But then he switched sides, probably because his wife's relatives, including the prominent headman Corn Tassel, began to advocate peace with the United States, and by 1778, in a complete reversal, he was fighting alongside them on the American side. Critics charged that Joseph Martin, a prominent Indian agent, politician, and militia general in the late eighteenth century, defended Indian land rights and compromised frontier security because he had married Cherokee Betsey Ward and grown close to her family.[102] And as Andrew Jackson made his first attempt to convince the Cherokees to move west of the Mississippi in 1817, he complained bitterly that Colonel Gideon Morgan, who had led Cherokee troops in the Creek war, had "lately taken to wife a native of this nation, and he declares, he does not wish to live under the laws of our country, that he prefers cherokee Government."[103] The readiness with which intermarried white men became Indians or, at least, sided with Indians caused alarm among Anglo-Americans, especially as their numbers increased and their children grew up in Indian communities.

When intermarried white men behaved inappropriately, Native people took steps to reign them in. After 1800, many of the non-

Indian men who married Native women did so in anticipation of
financial gain through access to land and proceeds from land cessions. A Cherokee land cession in 1817 provided for emigration
west of the Mississippi and awarded reservations, tracts of land
within the ceded territory, to individuals. Some people clearly regarded land cession and emigration as an opportunity to profit personally. The first eight people who registered for reservations were
white men, each of whom signed "in right of his wife." Altogether
approximately 20 percent of the reservations went to white men. [104]
Cherokee women met and sent a petition to the national council
protesting land sales in general and "some white men" in particular. They pointed out that these men had lived in the Cherokee
Nation since their youth, married Cherokee women, and sired large
families. "These ought to be our truest friends but prove our worst
enemies," the women wrote. "They seem to be only concerned how
to increase their riches, but do not care what becomes of our Nation,
nor even of their own wives and children." [105] This petition almost
certainly contributed to the council's decision in 1819 to cede no
more land and to accept no further reservations.

Unfamiliar with the Native practice of married men and women
holding property separately, some white men in the early nineteenth century hoped to use state laws, which did not recognize the
property rights of married women, to gain control of their wives'
estates. [106] Consequently, Indian nations took steps to prevent op-
portunistic marriages. In 1819 the Cherokees limited a white man
to one wife, required him to get a license to wed, and specified that
his Cherokee wife's property "shall not be subject to the disposal
of her husband, contrary to her consent." [107] By 1825, the Creeks
had passed a law that if a white man left his Indian wife, "he shall
leave all his property with his children for their support." They
also took measures to recognize formally the separate property of
married men and women and to limit the entry of whites into the

nation.[108] In passing such laws, southern Indians codified some existing practices and modified others, but their intent—forcing white men to conform to the rules of Native societies—reflected the reality of more than a century of intermarriage.

By the first decade of the nineteenth century, hundreds of white people, mostly men, lived in the southern Indian nations. Caleb Swan estimated Creek population in 1790 at twenty-five to twenty-six thousand. Each of the fifty-two Creek towns had at least one trader, several had more than one, and each trader employed one or two packhorse men. In addition, every town had one or two white families not engaged in trading who had "fled from some part of the frontier, to this asylum of liberty." Whites in the Creek Nation totaled nearly three hundred, which Swan considered "a number sufficient to contaminate all the natives."[109] Swan's remark was a cultural not a genetic assessment, but the extent of intermarriage, particularly with the English, was obvious to Bernard Romans, who remarked that "before the English traders came among them, there were scarcely any half breed, but now they abound among the younger sort."[110] In 1809, United States Agent Return J. Meigs counted 341 intermarried whites in the Cherokee Nation; Cherokees numbered 12,395. The removal roll of 1835 reported 211 intermarried whites; "mixed bloods" counted for slightly less than 23 percent of the population.[111] Chickasaws and Choctaws had a comparable percentage of whites and their descendants.[112]

According to Benjamin Hawkins, the man responsible for implementing the "civilization" program that the United States government adopted in the 1790s to culturally transform Indians into Anglo-Americans, their influence was largely negative. Writing specifically about the "Indian countrymen" who had entered Native territory during the Revolution, he characterized them as "lazy, cunning, thievish animal[s], so much degraded in the estimation of the Indians that they are considered a slave of their family and treated accordingly." Indeed, Hawkins regarded these men as an impediment to his mission and contended that "the plan [of civilization], since it begins to develop itself and be understood, takes root every where better among the Indians who have had no white people connected with them than where they have."[113] While Hawkins grossly overstated his case, he recognized that the white men who made their homes in Indian country and married Indian women had far less effect on Native people than the Indians had on them. In many ways, they had chosen to become Indians, and this choice rankled Hawkins and other "civilizers." Ignorant of long-established traditions of matrilineal kinship and chiefly power, Hawkins tended to regard Native societies as culturally impoverished and socially malleable. In his view, the superior, more complex culture of Anglo-Americans should have won out over the inferior, simplistic, debased culture of Native peoples. Native people, he believed, should follow the cultural and political leadership of the white men in their midst. Instead, they incorporated Indian countrymen into their own social, economic, and political system. Native people, in other words, did the molding, and the result was Indians who looked like white men and enjoyed some of the accouterments of Euro-American life but whose loyalties rested squarely with the Native nations into which they had married. At the end of the eighteenth century, southern Indian country probably looked racially and ethnically diverse, thanks to all those whites who had married "in the Indian manner," but a bedrock of Native culture underlay and held together the disparate elements that made up the social landscape.

Benjamin Hawkins and the Creek Indians.

Painting by an unidentified artist, c. 1805.

Greenville County Museum of Art, Greenville, S.C.

Gift of the Museum Association, Inc.

The Chief Vann House, Chatsworth, Ga.
Georgia Department of Natural Resources,
Historic Preservation Division.

William McIntosh, "mixed blood" Creek.
From Thomas McKenney and James Hall, *History of the Indian Tribes
of North America*. From the copy in The Rare Book Collection,
The University of North Carolina at Chapel Hill.

Major Ridge, "full-blood" Cherokee.
From Thomas McKenney and James Hall, *History of the Indian Tribes of North America*. From the copy in The Rare Book Collection, The University of North Carolina at Chapel Hill.

CHAPTER TWO

"Both White and Red"

Biracial People in Indian Society

In 1768, a group of Cherokee headmen met British emissaries at
Hard Labour Creek to negotiate a land cession. The great war chief
Oconostota addressed the assembly and described an increasingly
common situation. The British deputy superintendent of Indian
affairs, a man named Alexander Cameron, had, Oconostota announced, "got a son by a Cherokee woman." Cameron, whom the
Cherokee headman referred to as "beloved brother," had been a
trustworthy interpreter of English words and deeds for the Cherokees. Moreover, he was able to explain the Cherokee position on
issues to the British, and the Cherokees hoped that the son would
someday replace the father in this capacity: "We are desirous,"
Oconostota continued, "that he may educate the boy like the white
people, and cause him to be able to read and write, that he may
resemble both white and red, and live among us when his father
is dead." The Cherokees were willing to invest even further in
the young man's future: "We have given him for this purpose a
large piece of land, which we hope will be agreeable to our father [the king]."[1] In fact, the gift was not "agreeable" to the king.
British law provided that only the government, and not individuals,

receive title to land from Indian tribes, a principle that southern Indians normally respected and that the United States subsequently adopted. Consequently, Oconostota precipitated a diplomatic crisis by making a special provision for Cameron's son, whom the British considered to be a compatriot since the boy's father was British.[2] This apparent violation of British law placed Cameron's job in jeopardy until his superior intervened and explained that the Cherokees regarded Cameron's son as Cherokee, not British, because his mother was Cherokee and because paternity, in Cherokee culture, played no role in determining ethnicity or nationality. The grant of land was merely a gift to one of their own. The Cherokees recognized that Cameron's son had opportunities not normally available to young Cherokee men, but, while they encouraged his father to "educate the boy like the white people, that he may resemble both white and red," his maternal connection to the Cherokees, symbolized by the gift of land and the right to live among them, made him a Cherokee.

Cameron was not alone in fathering a child by a Native woman. The number of mixed race children in southern Indian societies increased dramatically throughout the eighteenth and early nineteenth centuries, and some of those children came to play enormously significant roles in their tribes as wealthy planters and powerful chiefs. Many non-Indian contemporaries and even some modern historians have attributed their success to their European ancestry, and explanations for their achievements range from the superiority of white "blood" over Indian "blood" to the influence of white fathers on their lives. We can dismiss the first explanation as the product of nineteenth-century scientific racism; modern scholars reject the notion of a racial hierarchy, and they know that "blood" does not determine behavior. The second explanation is more defensible, but it too is problematic. Most intermarried white men lived like Indians, and they raised their children as Indians.[3]

And while some of them sought an elementary English education for their offspring, so did a number of Native men who had no European ancestry. It was Oconostota, after all, not Cameron, who publicly proposed educating Cameron's son. Even if we reject both of these explanations, our historical gaze has fastened on the ways in which these "mixed blood" children lived like whites—their dress, their houses, their market orientation, their conversions to Christianity, and their political innovations that transformed southern Indian tribes into republics. But we need to shift our gaze and look at the children of interracial unions in a Native context as well, in order to understand fully how they became "both white and red."

The identity of Cameron's son as a Cherokee rested on the Cherokees' matrilineal kinship system, probably the feature of Native culture in the Southeast that Europeans found most perplexing. In a matrilineal kinship system, a person's only blood relatives are those on the mother's side. Southeastern Indians—Cherokees, Chickasaws, Choctaws, Creeks, and virtually all other Native people in the region—did not consider fathers and fathers' families to be the blood relatives of children. Consequently, the progeny of Native women and white men had no formal kin ties to their fathers, and a father had no right to exercise any authority over his children. The responsibility for support, education, and discipline fell to the mother's family, and the individual who performed many of the functions Europeans associated with fatherhood was the maternal uncle, or mother's brother. Few white men were able to usurp this central role in their children's lives, and when, like Cameron, they did so, it was only by permission of their in-laws.

As early as the first decade of the eighteenth century, European men began to experience the anguish that often accompanied such vastly different expectations of fatherhood. John Lawson, the naturalist who traveled through piedmont Carolina in 1701, generally regarded relationships with Indian women in a favorable light—

they provided sex, language instruction, food, intelligence, and protection—but he did identify "one great Misfortune." The children
of European men and Native women often received no education
except "in a State of Infidelity." Lawson recognized that matrilineal
kinship was responsible: "The Children always fall to the Women's
Lot; for it often happens that two *Indians* that have liv'd together as
Man and Wife; in which Time they have had several Children; if
they part, and another Man possess her, all the Children go along
with the Mother, and none with the Father." Native people understood and accepted this way of reckoning kin, but problems
arose when European men sought to assert patriarchal authority:
"It ever seems impossible," Lawson observed, "for the Christians to
get their Children (which they have by these *Indian* Women) away
from them; whereby they might bring them up in the Knowledge
of the Christian Principles."[4]

Most European men who married into Native societies remained
on the periphery of their children's lives. At the end of the eighteenth century, United States agent Benjamin Hawkins lamented:
"The traders, several of whom have amassed considerable fortunes,
have almost all of them been as inattentive of their children as the
Indians."[5] The parents of Catharine Brown, an early convert to
Christianity, both had white fathers, but, according to missionaries, "they were brought up like others of their nation;—no better
acquainted with the language, religion, manners, or customs of the
white people."[6] In some cases, the level of fathers' disinterest in
their children's upbringing was truly astonishing. John Norton, a
Mohawk who visited relatives in the Cherokee Nation in the first
decade of the nineteenth century, encountered a Scottish trader
who lived with his wife and children, some of whom were adults,
but could not converse with them. "I thought it singular," Norton
wrote with understatement, "that this old man should neither have
taught his family to speak English, nor that he himself had learned
of them to speak Cherokee."[7]

Fathers who sought to take an active role in their children's lives often found themselves thwarted. In the late eighteenth century, the naturalist William Bartram encountered an elderly white trader, James Germany, who had been married to a Creek woman for many years. Bartram described the trader's wife as "of a very amiable and worthy character and disposition, industrious, prudent and affectionate." As in all Creek households, however, Mrs. Germany had control of the children because they belonged to her family, not to Mr. Germany's. The father wanted to send them to Savannah or Charleston for their education. According to Bartram, the trader had "accumulated a pretty fortune by his industry and commendable conduct," and he no doubt wanted his children, especially his sons, educated in the English language and the principles of accounting. Mr. Germany, however, could not "prevail upon his wife to consent to it." And, of course, he could not send his children to school without their mother's permission.[8]

When the American Board of Commissioners for Foreign Missions, an interdenominational organization headquartered in Boston, established a mission among the Cherokees in 1818, the missionaries had to deal constantly with the authority of mothers over children. In one incident, a father, whom they described as "a halfbreed of some education," enrolled his three children in the mission school. The children had two different mothers, neither of whom was still married to the father, and all three parents had remarried. In bringing the children to the mission, the father had grossly overstepped his bounds. Soon the mother of two of the children appeared, removed them from school, and told the missionaries that the mother of the third was coming for her child as well. Although they had only recently arrived in the Cherokee Nation, the missionaries understood that the mothers were simply exercising their prerogative. "The mothers among this people," they explained to their board, "are considered as having a right to the children in preference to the fathers." Missionaries quickly learned to consult mothers about their plans for their children. When preparations were being made for John Ridge, the son of a "full-blood" headman who advocated acculturation, to attend school in Connecticut, the missionaries specifically "enquired if his mother was willing" to have him go.[9] Not only was she willing, she considered his education to be her responsibility and sold some of her own livestock to finance his endeavor.

Refusal to surrender the governance of children to wives and in-laws made a white man a decidedly unattractive spouse for Native women. Not long after Benjamin Hawkins arrived at the Creek Agency on the Flint River west of Macon, Georgia, the matriarch of a prominent Creek family paid him a visit and offered him her daughter, a young widow with three small children, for his wife. At this point, Hawkins had not yet decided if he would marry a Native woman—ultimately he did not—but he already knew about some of the pitfalls of such a liaison. Creek women, he had learned, "were in the habit of assuming and exercising complete rule, such as it was, over their children, and not attending to the advice of their white husbands." On the chance that he might decide to accept the mother's offer, he wanted to make sure that no such difficulties arose. Consequently, he wrote a note to mother and daughter, and then read it aloud to them. He complimented the young woman on her appearance and her "fine children" and noted that she was "of good family." Then he issued an ultimatum: "If I do, if it is for a single night, and she has a child, I shall expect it will be mine, that I may clothe it and bring it up as I please." Furthermore, Hawkins insisted on the governance of step-children: "the wife must consent that I shall clothe them, feed them, and bring them up as I please, and no one of her family shall oppose my doing so." The old woman balked at Hawkins's conditions: "She would not consent that the women and children should be under the direction of the father, and the negotiation ended there."[10]

Hawkins again confronted the power of the maternal family when he sought to assume control of the orphan daughters of Alexander McGillivray, a Creek "mixed blood" headman who attempted to centralize tribal government in the 1780s and negotiated the first Creek treaty with the United States in 1790. A prominent merchant in Pensacola, at whose house McGillivray died in 1793, managed to send the headman's son to Scotland, the country of McGillivray's father, to be educated (and die). The two daughters went to live with their Creek uncle. Hawkins offered "to bring up the daughters under my own roof, to fit them for acts of usefulness, and particularly to fit them to be instrumental in civilizing their brethren." But Hawkins failed: "Their family did not accord with the idea and the custom of the nation forced otherwise."[11]

Hawkins had assumed that a Scottish grandfather linked the McGillivray children to British culture and that they were, in modern parlance, bicultural. From the perspective of the Creeks and other southern Indians, however, the concepts of "bicultural" or "mixed race" simply did not exist. If a person's mother was Creek, then that person was Creek, regardless of who the father was, and many descendants of Indians and whites chose to live as Indians, challenging the attempt of Hawkins and others to link culture and race. Louis-Philippe, who visited the Cherokees while he was in exile during the French Revolution, recognized that the Cherokees had no special category for the children of white men and Indian women. "The family is reckoned around women rather than men as in our society," he wrote. "In consequence, the children of white men and Indian women are Indians like the others." Louis-Philippe realized, however, that whites did not regard these children in the same way as the Cherokees did: "The Americans call them *half breeds*." The Frenchman had heard, probably from his white traveling companions, that they were "a bit more intelligent than the others," but he saw nothing to distinguish them from Cherokees who had no European ancestry: "They live precisely as the others do, neither read nor write, and ordinarily speak only the tribal tongue."[12]

These children were Indians because their blood relatives, their mothers' families, were Indians, and the primary male influence on their lives came from maternal uncles. The historical record is replete with references to close relationships between uncles and nephews. Uncles who were in positions of authority entrusted nephews with important diplomatic and military missions. The Creek Wolf King sent his nephew to meet with David Taitt in 1772 because he was not able to ride long distances, the nephew of an Abika headman accompanied a Cherokee captive home and engaged in peace negotiations, and the nephew of Yamacraw chief Tomochichi, who is featured with his uncle in a famous portrait, led a war party against St. Augustine to avenge the deaths of two Yamacraws on Amelia Island.[13] In all of these examples, uncles were grooming and positioning nephews for leadership roles. Uncles also took care of nephews in more mundane ways. A man from Fusihatchi, for example, complained to David Taitt about a British trader who had stolen four horses from his nephew.[14] And finally, the community turned to uncles when heart-rending decisions had to be made. A young man in Coweta killed the brother of the resident trader, who threatened to leave the town if the murderer was not punished. The chiefs conferred, and ultimately, "the uncle of the murderer said that he [the trader] should have satisfaction."[15] No court, even one composed of chiefs, decided this issue; the man's uncle did. Rather than have the responsibility for the death fall on another clan, members of the murderer's clan carried out the execution.

Political power normally passed from uncle to nephew according to matrilineal lines of descent.[16] Thomas Nairne observed that "The Savages reckon all their fameiles from the mothers side, and have not the least regard for who is their father. . . . For this reason the Chiefs sisters son alwais succeeds, and never his own."[17] John Lawson found the same practice in eastern North Carolina: "The Succession falls not to the King's Son but to his Sister's Son, which is a sure way to prevent Imposters in the Succession."[18] At the end of the eighteenth century, according to Hawkins, upon the death of a Creek chief, "if his nephews are fit for the office, one of them takes his place as his successor; if they are unfit, one is chosen from the next of kin, the descent is always in the female line."[19] When chiefs deviated from the established practice, as they sometimes did, trouble erupted. The Dog Lieutenant of Autossee, a Creek town, tried to return a British commission he had received because his uncle "wanted to have the Commission given to his son." The Dog Lieutenant, a high-ranking headman, told David Taitt that "he did not Like to be at variance with his Uncle." That is, he was willing to sacrifice this honor to maintain good relations. The uncle was fully aware that he was behaving inappropriately, and when Taitt visited his town, "he went and hid himself being ashamed of the dispute between them."[20]

The strong bond between uncles and nephews extended to the sons of white men. White fathers almost certainly had more sway over their children than most Native fathers did, but uncles still played an important role. In the mid-eighteenth century the sister of Old Tassel, the principal chief of the upper Cherokees, married a white trader who had served as an interpreter for the British in the Seven Years' War. Old Tassel died in 1788, killed under a flag of truce by Tennessee militia, but his prestige reflected on other members of his family, including his sister's son, John Watts. Following the American Revolution, Watts and another uncle, Doublehead, Old Tassel's brother, joined the Chickamauga towns in northwestern Georgia in their resistance against the United States and the encroachments of white settlers. When the Chickamauga war chief,

Dragging Canoe, died in 1792, John Watts and Doublehead were the leading candidates to replace him. The Cherokees chose war chiefs primarily on the basis of merit, but kin ties to prominent families also played a role. Watts won out, perhaps because he advocated the continuation of hostilities against whites when other leaders, who had no English ancestry, urged negotiation.[21] Even after the Chickamaugas made peace in 1794, Watts continued to play a prominent role in Cherokee politics. Louis-Philippe, who traveled through the Cherokee Nation in 1797, described him as "the Nation's greatest warrior and is considered the most influential of the chiefs . . . whose views always prevail in council."[22] The Cherokees listened to Watts because of his accomplishments, not his ancestry, but his Cherokee uncles provided him with the kind of training and experience that made his achievements possible.

The political skills that Native leaders needed changed dramatically at the end of the eighteenth century. For most of the century, southern Indians had engaged in play-off diplomacy, negotiating or threatening to negotiate with more than one European power and using imperial rivalries to maintain their political autonomy. With the expulsion of the French from North America in 1763 at the end of the French and Indian War and the defeat of the British in the American Revolution, southern Indians had only two potential allies and trading partners—Spain and the United States. The Spanish empire was on the wane, and although all southern Indians conducted some trade and diplomacy with Spain, the United States was clearly the power to be reckoned with. Of particular concern was American expansionism, both the legally sanctioned extension of the frontier through the purchase of Indian land and the illegal encroachments on tribal domains by white hunters, traders, and settlers. The invasion of the Chickamauga towns in the early 1790s ended military resistance in the South, and the defeat of the Indian alliance in the Old Northwest demonstrated to southern Indians that even concerted action was futile. Diplomacy and accommodation promised the best hope for stemming the tide of white settlement and protecting the homelands of southern Indians.[23] Family connections and traditional accomplishments continued to matter, but familiarity with Anglo-American customs, some knowledge of English, an openness to culture change, and a steadfast resolve to resist land cessions also became important considerations in the choice of leaders.

The first three decades of the nineteenth century were a period of political turmoil and innovation for southern Indians. Under increasing pressure to sell their lands and move west of the Mississippi, they resisted these demands by centralizing their governments, granting their chiefs and councils greater power, and enacting laws that protected both individual and tribal property. In the process, serious divisions emerged. The Cherokees temporarily deposed their principal chief in 1808 in order to prevent the division of their nation, and in 1827 they put down a rebellion against constitutional government. The Creeks fought a civil war in 1813–14 brought on in large part by differences over acculturation (this division contributed to the emergence of the Seminoles as a distinct tribe), and in 1825 the Creek national council ordered the execution of a chief who illegally ceded land. The Choctaws replaced their district chiefs in 1826 with men who favored centralization and resistance to removal.

In these years, the sons and grandsons of intermarried white men came increasingly to the fore, tempting Anglo-Americans to depict internal dissention and conflict in racial terms, but most outbreaks of violence defied racial explanation. Like many Anglo-Americans of the period, Benjamin Hawkins tried desperately to understand the Creek War, which erupted in 1813 and brought General Andrew Jackson to national prominence, as a conflict between Indians and "half breeds," but his own accounting of participants on each side belied this interpretation. He acknowledged that the "Red Sticks," the people he regarded as enemy Indians, opposed to whites and "mixed bloods," included one hundred whites and eighty African Americans.[24] A number of their leaders, including William Weatherford, Josiah Francis, and Peter McQueen, descended from white men and Creek women.[25] Although some of the warriors whom Hawkins regarded as loyal had European ancestry, most of those who attempted to put down the insurrection did not.[26] Rather than attempt to understand the civil war in economic, political, and religious terms, as most modern scholars do, Hawkins saw it only in terms of race.[27]

Participants in other conflicts among southern Indians also fail to conform to a strictly racial interpretation. When the "mixed blood" Choctaws David Folsom and Greenwood LeFlore came to power in the eastern and western districts in 1826, they displaced one "full-blood" chief, Mushulatubbee, and one "mixed blood," Robert Cole. Furthermore, the chiefs who ranked just below Folsom and LeFlore in the political hierarchy were "full-bloods," and among the most ardent supporters of Mushulatubbee were the "mixed bloods," Peter and James Pitchlynn.[28] Among the Creeks, "mixed blood" William McIntosh was only too willing to accept bribes from United States treaty commissioners in the early 1820s for agreeing to sell Creek lands, but "mixed blood" John Ross exposed him rather than accept a similar arrangement in the sale of Cherokee lands. When McIntosh became the first signatory on the illegal Treaty of Indian Springs in 1825 that ceded Creek lands in Georgia, Etommee Tustenuggee, a "full-blood," became the second. The Creek principal chief Big Warrior, a "full-blood," denounced McIntosh and endorsed his execution as did the second ranking chief Opothle Yoholo, a "mixed blood," and when the Creeks executed McIntosh, Etommee Tustenuggee died at his side.[29]

Neither side in any of these conflicts consisted exclusively of one racial group or the other, but in all factions, leadership roles increasingly fell to men with white ancestry. Many had skills that changing circumstances demanded. A number of these new "mixed blood" leaders—but certainly not all—spoke English, and some had received a formal education. For five years, Choctaw Greenwood LeFlore lived in Nashville where he attended school, while his countryman David Folsom enrolled in a common school for six months, long enough to master basic literacy and arithmetic.[30] Peter Pitchlynn attended Choctaw Academy in Kentucky, a school that accepted students from a number of tribes, including the Creeks who generally opposed schools within their nation.[31] Cherokee John Ross had a private tutor and studied at a Presbyterian mission school.[32] Creek David Moniac became the first non-white cadet at the United States Military Academy at West Point.[33] In addition to formal educational opportunities, most sons of white fathers and grandfathers learned about the political system of the United States from treaty commissioners and agents, who often relied on Indian countrymen as translators. Some white fathers subscribed to newspapers and bought books, and many taught their sons the principles of accounting. In a few cases, fathers may have intentionally prepared their sons to become leaders, but economic success was their primary focus. The path to political power lay with their sons' maternal kin, especially their uncles.

Tracing maternal lines for early-nineteenth-century Indian leaders is enormously difficult because contemporaries tended to record only paternity, but the individuals whose maternal relatives are known suggest that clan, lineage, and the influence of maternal relatives played an important role in their rise to prominence. The Choctaws provide the best example. Robert Cole succeeded his uncle Puckshunubbee as chief of the Choctaw's Western District only to be ousted by his nephew Greenwood LeFlore; David Folsom, who replaced Mushulatubbee as chief of the Eastern Division

in 1826, was the son of former chief Miko Pushkush's niece, that
is, of his clan and lineage; and Peter and James Pitchlynn, the
"mixed bloods" opposed to Folsom, were the nephews of Mushulatubbee.[34] Among the Creeks, Alexander McGillivray, the most
powerful chief in the nation in the late eighteenth century, was the
nephew of the Coushatta chief Red Shoes, who distinguished himself in raids on Spanish settlements and received from them a medal
acknowledging his power.[35] In the next generation, McGillivray's
nephew, William Weatherford, became a Red Stick leader in the
civil war. The tradition of power passing from uncle to nephew continued even after removal. George Harkins, nephew of Greenwood
LeFlore, followed his maternal uncle as chief of the Western District of the Choctaw Nation in 1830 and continued in that position
long after removal, and William Potter Ross succeeded his maternal uncle John Ross as principal chief of the Cherokee Nation in
1866.[36] White or "mixed blood" fathers, therefore, were not solely
responsible for the rise to power of a new generation of leaders;
maternal kin, especially uncles, played an important role.

Traditional notions of leadership enabled "mixed blood" leaders
to acquire and retain political positions. George Colbert, son of a
white man and his Chickasaw wife, because he had proven himself
as a warrior, became second only to Tishomingo, the Chickasaw
Great Warrior and leader of the Tchuckafalayah moiety that mo-
nopolized relations with the United States. In the American Revolution, Colbert fought Virginians near the mouth of the Ohio River
and Spaniards on the lower Mississippi as a member of Chickasaw
war parties. After the war, Colbert's Tchuckafalayah moiety supported the United States, and he and his brother joined a Chickasaw expedition that accompanied General Arthur St. Clair's ill-
fated campaign against the northwestern Indian alliance in 1791.
Once he had proven himself as a warrior, his prominence in his
moiety and in the nation rose.[37] War alone did not propel men

into leadership positions, but success in battle was certainly one of the popular expectations for chiefs. Many of the Cherokees' national leaders in the 1820s, for example, had fought in the Creek war alongside the United States. These included Charles Hicks and John Ross, who became principal chiefs; Sequoyah, the inventor of the Cherokee syllabary; and Major Ridge, who led the Treaty Party in the 1830s. Understanding the importance of war honors to Native political leadership, the United States awarded the elderly Cherokee principal chief Pathkiller the rank of colonel.[38]

The rising generation of leaders brought to their new roles a concept of political authority that came from their mother's people. Among southern Indians, chiefs did not command their subjects. Instead, they gave voice to consensus and led only as long as their people had confidence in them. When the Choctaws deposed their old chiefs in 1826, they did so largely because the previous year two of them had agreed to the Treaty of Washington, which ceded Choctaw land in Arkansas, and used some of the proceeds to extinguish the debts of the signatories. The "mixed blood" chiefs who replaced them had traditional lineage claims on their positions and either denounced treaty provisions or had no role in its making. These new chiefs also drew on ancient symbols of power to validate their ascension and their decisions. When they made substantial changes to the Choctaw political system, for example, they held the council in the shadow of Nanih Waiya, the mound that had given birth to the Choctaws.[39] In 1808 the Cherokees cast out of office a "full-blood" chief who favored land cessions, and then as soon as the crisis passed, they restored him because in other ways his views reflected those of his people.[40] Two decades later, Cherokee chief John Ross, a "mixed blood," reflected the consensus of the vast majority of the Cherokee people in opposition to removal. Had he done otherwise, he would almost certainly have been impeached, as were three leaders of the minority faction, two "mixed bloods"

and a "full-blood," that promoted a removal treaty.[41] Chiefs, therefore, had power that they ultimately derived from the people, and
the people followed chiefs who represented their will as well as
demonstrated talents that they regarded as important.

Southeastern Indians traditionally linked military, political, and
spiritual power, a practice dating at least to the Mississippian cultural tradition that flourished in the Southeast from about A.D. 800.
Mississippian societies were hierarchical, and the elite based its
claim to authority on military might and spiritual power.[42] Chiefs
symbolically expressed their power by building their houses and
temples atop large earthen mounds and monopolizing exotic goods.
The collapse of Mississippian culture in the aftermath of the European invasion compromised this hierarchy, but chiefs retained
symbols of chiefly power, including a range of goods not normally
available to others. At the beginning of the eighteenth century,
John Lawson observed that "some of their great Men, as Rulers
and such, that have Plenty of Deer Skins by them, will often buy
the English-made Coats, which they wear on Festivals and other
Days of Visiting."[43] The coats were exotic. They came from the
chaotic world beyond the tribal domain, a world that possessed
great spiritual power and substantial danger. By wearing the coats,
chiefs demonstrated their command of these forces and their place
in any residual hierarchy. For this reason, European goods took
on significance beyond their material value, at least until they became widely available. In regulating the trade, as chiefs did until at
least the mid–eighteenth century, they controlled access to foreign
goods and spiritual power, and in the process, they secured their
own positions.[44]

The role that exotic goods and wealth played in making chiefly
power visible generally escaped the notice of eighteenth-century
observers, who extolled the economic egalitarianism of southeastern Indian societies, but William Bartram did note that a chief's

house differed from others in "being larger according as his ability or private riches may enable him." A chief received no tribute from the residents of his town, but he controlled the public granary and received presents from visitors.[45] While a chief may not have personally owned these goods, they were at his disposal, and his authority rested on his ability to provide for the material welfare of his people and extend hospitality to visitors. Southern Indians continued this Mississippian practice well into the nineteenth century and, in some settings, such as stomp grounds, into the twenty-first. In the late eighteenth century, the Seminole Cowkeeper, who owned large herds of cattle (hence his name), was able to draw on his personal wealth to perform the obligatory acts of hospitality when William Bartram visited him. According to Bartram, he "ordered some of the best steers of his droves to be slaughtered for a general feast for the whole town, in compliment of our arrival."[46] Personal wealth and communal wealth were not always distinguishable, and in order to demonstrate their chiefly power, chiefs had to provide appropriate feasts or risk compromising their prestige.

Cowkeeper and his Mississippian ancestors probably would have regarded as comfortingly familiar the scene that John Howard Payne described in 1840, the year after removal, when he visited Cherokee chief John Ross at his home in what is today eastern Oklahoma. Ross never locked his house, and large numbers of visitors constantly called on him. Ross had an obligation as chief to make sure that they had shelter and food. "At night," Payne wrote, "if two fourpost bedsteads in each of the two main rooms, on the ground floor, are insufficient for the guests, beds are spread in the center." Meals were quite a production: "As many as the table can accommodate, sit down indiscriminately. . . . set after set is summoned, till all are satisfied. The housekeeper never knows here whether she has to lodge and feed twenty-five or fifty or double the number."[47]

Ross, a highly acculturated, wealthy "mixed blood," fully satisfied ancient expectations of chiefs.

European policies often gave headmen command of economic resources and reinforced both chiefly authority and redistribution. Colonial officials typically presented gifts to chiefs in order to cement alliances.[48] Keeping an inequitable amount as a symbol of their authority and a hedge against future demands, chiefs redistributed goods to their followers. In 1717 the South Carolina House of Commons appropriated funds to buy "One Gun, one Cutlash and Belt, a Cagg Rum, a stript Duffield Blanket, a Peece Calicoe and some String Beads" for each of three visiting Cherokee headmen.[49] The gifts were not inconsequential; these goods were worth roughly sixty deerskins or about twice the annual kill of an average Cherokee hunter. When Hawkins arrived in the Creek Nation at the end of the eighteenth century, he complained about the "antient habits instilled . . . by French or British agents, that the red chiefs are to live on presents from their white friends."[50] While chiefs redistributed some of the gifts they received to members of their community, especially warriors, they also kept goods as symbols of chiefly authority, just as their Mississippian forebears had done. Consequently, powerful chiefs accumulated considerable wealth.

The United States tried to end gift-giving, but the new nation's procedure for paying for ceded lands served many of the same purposes. The United States adopted the British policy of dealing with Indian nations through treaties, which recognized both their legitimate claims to the soil and their sovereignty. Early treaties tried to force Indians to part with their land, but George Washington's administration insisted that Indians agree to cessions and receive compensation, a position that became enormously controversial in the 1820s.[51] Compensation came in the form of annuities, an annual payment of goods and/or cash. Annuities were mortgage payments, not gifts, but their distribution took the same form. Chiefs received them, kept some for themselves for personal and community use, and disbursed the rest to their constituents.[52] Control of the annuities, like gifts, was a prerogative of chiefs. Even if Hawkins did not recognize the similarity, Native people did. A Creek headman, Efau Hadjo, told Hawkins: "In old times when I visited Col. Stuart (the British superintendent) he would always give me what was sufficient for myself and my particular friends. I could get a piece of strouds or blankets, a bag of sugar or salt, some rum and coffee." Efau Hadjo knew that things had changed since the Americans defeated the British, but he also understood that headmen still enjoyed certain rights: "I know the amount of the stipend [annuity] allowed our town, and that allowed the Great Medal Chief and principal men of the town." He already had made advances against the annuity, a kind of redistribution on credit, and now he sought repayment: "Our Micco before he died last year told me when these things came to apply to you and receive them for some debts due to me from the town and the Chiefs and I have come to you for an order on them accordingly."[53]

The negotiation of treaties and payment for land through annuities were only part of United States Indian policy. Washington and his secretary of war, Henry Knox, also proposed the cultural transformation of Indians, and the federal government invested considerable resources in accomplishing this goal. Two considerations shaped this policy. The first was altruistic. Knox and Washington believed that if Indians did not give up their own way of life and adopt the customs and beliefs of their white neighbors, they were doomed. The Indians' only hope for survival, therefore, was "civilization." The second was more self-serving. The "civilization" program sought to turn Indians into yeoman farmers who would willingly sacrifice thousands of acres of hunting grounds in order to improve individual farmsteads with fences, barns, spinning wheels, looms, plows, livestock, and an array of consumer goods. Policy-makers defined "civilization" as commercial agriculture, English literacy, republican government, patriarchal families, Christianity, and most importantly, the "love for exclusive property" on which Knox believed "civilization" rested and the acquisition of Indian lands depended.[54] The government appointed agents to live among the Indians and to teach them, through example and instruction, how to live like whites. The most prominent of these agents was Benjamin Hawkins, who set up a model farm on the Flint River in 1796 and distributed spinning wheels, looms, plows, and other tools to the Creeks. Like their distribution of annuities, chiefs carefully controlled the implementation of the "civilization" program within their towns and used it to augment rather than undermine their authority. Headmen frequently applied to agents for spinning wheels, plows, and other goods, often specifying the individuals in their towns who needed them and explaining their circumstances, and then passed the items on to those who had requested them.[55]

The importance of the "civilization" program and United States agents in the lives of southern Indians, particularly in the early nineteenth century, affected the rise of "mixed blood" chiefs in subtle ways. Agents did not normally speak the language of the people whom they served, so they looked for employees and friends among Indians who spoke English. Most of these, of course, were "mixed bloods." Hawkins hired "mixed bloods" exclusively to carry the United States mail. They proved so reliable that he "directed such to be employed in all things wherein they can be useful to us."[56] Their close association with agents may have elevated the standing of some "mixed bloods" within their communities, at least in the first two decades of the nineteenth century. Alexander Cornells, for example, used his job at the agency to augment his authority as a chief; Cornells reminded another Creek that he was "a Chief of this land as well as himself and an interpreter."[57] In their acceptance of the material bounty of the "civilization" program and their cozy relationships with agents, headmen were fulfilling their traditional responsibility as chiefs to deal with outsiders and receive, in the name of the people, their largesse. Whatever affinity "mixed blood" chiefs had for "civilization" must be understood, at least in part, in the context of traditional expectations of chiefs.

Under the auspices of the "civilization" program, the federal government encouraged missionaries to set up schools and churches among southern Indians and, in 1819, established a "civilization" fund to underwrite these efforts. Just as they had with annuities and plows, chiefs sought to turn new religious ideas to their advantage. Chiefly authority in Mississippian culture had rested on spiritual claims and a monopoly of esoteric knowledge, and spiritual power had remained an essential component of leadership in the Southeast.[58] In the eighteenth century, for example, Bartram reported that The Long Warrior "was acknowledged by the Indians to have communion with powerful invisible beings or spirits and, on that account, esteemed worthy of homage and great respect."[59] When "mixed blood" chiefs and their "full-blood" colleagues welcomed missionaries and cultivated close ties to them, therefore, they not only took steps to prepare their people for the future, but they also asserted their role as spiritual leaders.

Native religion in the Southeast was an inclusive rather than an exclusive religion.[60] Southern Indians added new concepts and rituals, that is, new sources of spiritual power, to their religious life without necessarily abandoning or compromising their old beliefs. In 1765, for example, a Choctaw headman on a diplomatic mission to Mobile responded amiably to the cleric whose sermon he had recently heard: "Beloved Man, I will always[s] think well of this Friend of ours God Almighty whom you tell me so much of, and so let us drink to his health."[61] This man and other southern Indians, especially leaders, may have looked to Christianity to increase their power. Mastery of Christian principles sometimes elevated a person's standing in unexpected ways. In 1813 headman Charles Hicks became the second Cherokee to become a communicant member of the Moravian congregation at Spring Place in what is today north Georgia. Hicks, according to the Moravians, zealously tried to teach others about his new religious beliefs, but he had little success. In the process of discussion, however, he became extraordinarily well educated in traditional religion, and his knowledge on the subject was widely admired and sought.[62] Possessing such deep understanding could only have enhanced his prestige among Cherokees. In the Choctaw Nation, the earliest converts to Christianity were elderly men, those most likely to be priests and healers.[63] David Folsom, whose maternal uncle was one of the first Choctaw converts, used Christianity and Christian notions of morality to consolidate his political base, and his political opponents responded by becoming outspoken critics of the missionaries among the Choctaws. Far more was at issue in this contest than religion, but adversaries couched much of their rhetoric in religious terms.[64] Historian James Taylor Carson has observed that, for the Choctaws, "sacred and political power were inseparable," and the Christian camp meetings that Greenwood LeFlore and David Folsom "hosted became indistinguishable from their political councils."[65] By the late 1820s, most Cherokee, Chickasaw, and Choctaw headmen were nominal Christians, and the number of converts in these nations grew rapidly. After passage of the Indian Removal Act and the negotiation of removal treaties in 1830, however, Choctaws and Chickasaws left their churches in large numbers, perhaps because they questioned the power of this new religion to protect them from very real temporal dangers.[66]

While Creeks and Seminoles had little to do with Christian missions of any sort, Cherokees, Chickasaws, and Choctaws proved enthusiastic about the educational opportunities missionaries provided. Headmen saw schools as a boon to their power and competed for them. When the United Brethren or Moravians requested permission to open a school in the Cherokee Nation in the first decade of the nineteenth century, the national council tried to balance political interests by advising them to open two schools. The Moravians, however, put the question to the lot, their mechanism for making decisions, and built only near the home of headman James Vann. This decision, which the Cherokees viewed as political, contributed to the controversy in which the Moravians were embroiled for several years, but Vann, along with his son Joseph and son-in-law David McNair, served as loyal patrons to the school and basked in the glow of its eventual success.[67] Schools became a potent symbol of chiefly authority. When representatives of the American Board of Commissioners for Foreign Missions arrived in 1816, the council made sure that they built on the rejected site, the farmstead of John McDonald, maternal grandfather of John Ross, who lived nearby and became principal chief a decade later.[68] In 1820 a delegation of Presbyterians called on Chickasaw headman Levi Colbert to request permission to open a school. He directed them to locate near the Chickasaw agency and the Natchez Trace, sources of economic and political power and convenient to him and his family as well as to other "mixed blood" families concentrated there.[69] The various headmen in the Choctaw Nation vied for schools at their houses, a situation that, according to historian Clara Sue Kidwell, resulted in education "having little or no impact [on most Choctaws] because the mission schools were far removed from their villages."[70] For headmen, making reading, writing, and arithmetic available to large numbers of children was secondary to using the schools as an expression of their chiefly authority.

Because many of the leaders who advocated missions were "mixed bloods," ancestry appears to loom larger than it really did in Indians' support of schools. The heyday of missions in the Southeast was the decade of the 1820s, precisely the period in which many "mixed bloods" were coming of age and assuming leadership roles, but schools, in particular, found wide support that cannot be linked exclusively to ancestry. When missionaries arrived among the Choctaws in 1819, the three division chiefs, all of whom were "full-bloods," pledged a portion of their annuities and made personal donations to support the effort. When Pushmataha threatened to withdraw his $2000 several years later, it was because of his rivalry with another headman who had received a school, not fundamental opposition.[71] "Full-blood" headmen wanted the advantages of an English education for their descendants just as "mixed blood" headmen did. Puckshunubbee brought his nephew, whom the missionaries described as "a full-blooded wild Choctaw," to a mission school and signaled his awareness that times had changed and children needed new occupations: "We have no way at home to employ our children but to let them play. . . . I give him up to you to put him to a trade, or on the farm."[72] Ironically, Puckshunubbee's successor, "mixed blood" Robert Cole, had far less enthusiasm for schools than his uncle and predecessor and complained that missionaries turned young men into slaves by requiring them to work in the field.[73] When missionaries began teaching the children in the Choctaw language, the "full-blood" Mushulatubbee complained that they were not learning useful skills: "We have never received a Scholar out of their schools that was able to keep a Grog shop book."[74]

Missionaries, however, may have inadvertently bolstered the power of the "mixed bloods" by favoring them much as the agents did. The American Board of Commissioners for Foreign Missions explicitly targeted "mixed bloods" in its work among the Cherokees. "Those who will be the first educated," wrote the head of the mission, "will be the children of the halfbreeds and of the leading men of the nation."[75] Such favoritism simply increased the likeli-

hood that "leading men" would be "half-breeds" and contributed
to the enrollment of children with white ancestry in numbers disproportionate to "mixed bloods" in the population. Nevertheless,
many "mixed blood" children arrived with few skills. For example, Catharine Brown, the American Board's most widely publi-
cized convert, enrolled in the Brainerd mission school at present-
day Chattanooga when she was seventeen or eighteen and was
barely able to read. Jeremiah Evarts, treasurer of the American
Board, described her parents as "half-breeds," but neither spoke
English. After several months at the mission school, Evarts com-
pared Catharine favorably to schoolgirls in New England in terms
of her "complexion" and "features" as well as her "dress, pronun-
ciation, or manners." [76] For a young man, school attendance ultimately contributed to his prestige as an adult and his claim on
power. Cherokee John Ridge described the rising generation of
Cherokee leaders as being "of fine habits, temperate & genteel in
their deportment." An education, Ridge thought, also contributed
to the ability of young men to marry well: "The females aspire to
gain the affection of such men & to the females we may always
ascribe the honor of effecting the civilization of man." [77]

Just as "mixed bloods" were disproportionately represented in
government and mission schools, they also accounted for most
members of the economic elite in the Southeast. The avenues to
wealth were diverse enough in the eighteenth century that an
emerging economic elite was by no means composed exclusively
of the children of white men. [78] The naturalist William Bartram
met a Creek man named Boatswain whose family and African
American slaves cultivated nearly a hundred acres of fenced fields.
Boatswain had "acquired his riches by trading with the white people." He transported a number of Native products, including deerskins, other furs and hides, tallow, honey, and beeswax, to the
Altamaha River where he transferred the goods to boats. He then

descended the river to towns along the Georgia coast, sometimes traveling as far as Savannah, and traded his cargo for "*Sugar, Coffee & every other kind of goods suitable for the Indian Markets.*"[79]

Having a white father with substantial assets, however, clearly provided a material advantage. Among the white men who lived in Indian country, a number amassed sizeable estates and built houses that trader James Adair likened to "towers in cities, beyond the common size of those of the Indians."[80] Traders, colonial officials, loyalists in the American Revolution, and other whites who moved into Indian country often brought with them considerable property, particularly in the form of livestock and slaves, and their facility with European languages and markets enabled them to prosper. For example, James Logan Colbert arrived among the Chickasaws in 1729 with forty African American slaves, married into the nation, and established a plantation.[81] Louis Durant and the brothers Louis and Michael LeFlore, who came from Canada to trade with the Choctaws after France's defeat in the French and Indian War, introduced large cattle herds into the Choctaw Nation.[82] Although white fathers could not leave their children land, which tribes held in common, they did bequeath store inventories, livestock, and slaves.

In addition to the chattel property that white fathers left their children, "mixed bloods" also inherited the dwellings, stores, warehouses, and barns to which their Indian mothers, following Native custom and law that vested title to improved realty in matrilineages, had laid claim. Consequently, the descendants of Colbert, Durant, the LeFlores, and other similarly endowed white men were often very wealthy, and they used their wealth to expand their economic enterprises and to acquire many of the accouterments that their white neighbors associated with wealth. Some of the structures these "mixed blood" children built in Georgia still stand, among them, the red-brick, white-column house that Cherokee James Vann erected near what is today Chatsworth and the popular hotel that Creek William McIntosh operated at Indian Springs near Jackson. Vann, McIntosh, and other wealthy men were prominent in politics, and they inscribed their power on the landscape through the erection of elegant houses, much in the same way that their Mississippian ancestors did when they built temple mounds. Like the earthworks at Ocmulgee, Etowah, Nacoochee, and Kolomoki in Georgia; Moundville in Alabama; Nikwasi in North Carolina; and Nanih Waiya in Mississippi, the Vann house and McIntosh's tavern bear witness to the political and economic power of chiefs.

White fathers certainly contributed to the fortunes of Native elites in the early nineteenth century, but the wealth their children inherited did not necessarily continue to descend patrilineally. Under traditional inheritance patterns, a man's personal property went to his sisters and their children. When Alexander McGillivray, the son of a Scottish trader and a Creek woman, died in 1793, his sisters, Sehoy McPherson Tait Weatherford and Sophia McGillivray Durant, laid claim to his estate. They either destroyed their brother's belongings as a traditional act of grief or they conveyed his property, particularly slaves, to their own sons, whom they considered McGillivray's rightful heirs according to the long established principle of matrilineal descent. When McGillivray's half brother, Malcolm McPherson Jr., died in 1799, the same thing happened. Weatherford, Durant, and a third sister, Janet McGillivray Milfort Crook, sent warriors from their town to take what they believed was rightfully theirs, and they succeeded. In both cases, representatives of a powerful English trading firm in Pensacola tried to intervene on behalf of the deceased's sons, but public opinion in the Creek Nation clearly favored the women.[83] Similarly, the bulk of the estate of Cherokee William Shorey, son of a Tory and a Cherokee woman, went to the grandson of his sister, his traditional heir.[84] Consequently, a wealthy uncle was perhaps more desirable than a wealthy father.

"Mixed blood" offspring also acquired wealth in traditional Native pursuits, which they learned from maternal uncles. Hunters individually owned the skins of the deer they killed and profited personally from their sale. John Norton described how one of the Cherokee McIntoshes got his start: "In his youth, he was a great Hunter but now he follows trade and Agriculture. He has much the appearance of a Scotchman, and so he is, on his father's side, who was an officer at Fort Loudon."[85] In addition to profits from the deerskin trade, men acquired personal possessions from colonial officials who supplied them with guns, ammunition, rum, and other goods in exchange for their military service. A market in Indian slaves provided warriors with another opportunity to profit by selling their war captives rather than torturing or adopting them. The Indian slave trade had largely ended by the mid–eighteenth century, and the American Revolution obviated a European need for warriors, but new markets and demands emerged. Young men who found themselves with no way to win war honors or acquire guns and ammunition began to raid the frontier, seizing horses, slaves, and things of value.[86] Scalps and other war trophies had once marked their status as warriors, but now emblems of victory were indistinguishable from the measures of success employed by their white neighbors. Menawa, the "mixed blood" who led the party that executed the Creek William McIntosh in 1825, made his first fortune stealing horses from the Cumberland settlements in east Tennessee and then became a respectable planter and trader. When Creek society shattered into civil war in 1813, Menawa easily adapted the skills acquired in rustling horses to war and emerged as one of the few Red Stick survivors of the battle of Horseshoe Bend. Following the war, he gradually regained his wealth, which had been destroyed, and became prominent in Creek national politics. Moving easily between roles, he wore a United States military uniform for formal occasions, as befitted a warrior.[87] Other warriors, including the Cherokees John Watts and Doublehead, made an easy transition from warrior to planter and entrepreneur, and like these two, some had white fathers and some did not.

"Mixed blood" members of the elite may well have learned entrepreneurial skills and inherited some of their wealth from white fathers, but a subtle value change in eighteenth-century Native societies also contributed to their individualism and acquisitiveness. Before the advent of the deerskin trade and imperial rivalries, the economies of southern Indians rested on agriculture whose labor and rituals were communal. The Green Corn Ceremony that commemorated the new crop brought together the entire town to restore spiritual and social balance, ritualize shared values of community, equality, and harmony, and celebrate the crop and the communal labor that had produced it. War and hunting, by contrast, entailed an individualistic ethic: a man acted alone, even when he was a member of a group, to kill a deer or a person. Furthermore, the deerskin belonged to him individually, and although his clan might claim a captive or relish a war trophy, he sang alone of his personal exploits in the scalp dance. Colonial wars and the deerskin trade elevated the importance of these activities and the individualistic values associated with them. Hunters and warriors acquired goods, such as guns and knives, for their individual use, and they prized them as tokens of their individual success. The traditional practices of interring personal possessions with the owner and annually destroying surpluses at the Green Corn Ceremony had thwarted the emergence of an economic elite, but these practices waned as an enormous variety of goods became widely available. Guns, in particular, began to pass from one generation to the next. The grave of the war chief Oconostota, for example, contained beads, vermillion, an iron cup, a knife, eyeglasses, and stone pipes, but no gun.[88] Neither buried nor destroyed, goods accumulated, and southern Indians came to appreciate their value.

As historian Claudio Saunt has pointed out, they also increasingly bought locks to protect their possessions.[89]

Many southern Indians found it easy to divert their individualism and acquisitiveness to other pursuits. A Cherokee "mixed blood," Young Wolf, described how he amassed his substantial estate in a will he wrote in 1814: "By my being careful & by my own industry, I have gathered a smart chance of property, and my first start was from herding my brother's cattle. I recvd one calf which I took my start from, except my own industry, & with cow and calf which I sold, I bought two sows & thirteen pigs. Sometime after I was able to purchase three mares, & the increase of them since is amounted to thirty more or less & from that start I gathred money enough to purchase a negro woman named Tabb, also a negro man named Ceasar." In ruling on a case involving the family following Young Wolf's death, the National Council found that the widow, Janey Wolf, had operated the family's farm "with economy & propriety, and in consequence thereby has accumulated considerable money, by keeping a house of entertainment for travellers, which enabled her to purchase some Negroes." [90] Young Wolf's father was white, but that circumstance played little role in his accumulation of wealth. Instead, both he and his wife had invested profits wisely to expand their enterprises from one calf to a considerable estate.

The Wolfs were not alone in looking for opportunities to invest, and like Janey many of them took advantage of the roads that began criss-crossing southern Indian nations in the early nineteenth century. Chiefs had a decided advantage. The promise of inns and ferries actually induced many chiefs to agree to the roads that cut through their nations, and they obtained important concessions from the United States in treaties that permitted construction. Furthermore, headmen received permission from the councils in which they sat to operate stands (or inns), ferries, and additional toll roads. Within a decade after the Chickamauga Cherokees had made peace, the old warrior Doublehead received the rights to a ferry on the road between Augusta and Nashville and a contract to operate taverns. The agreement with the United States, signed in 1803, gave preference for other ferries to "persons having connections with the Cherokee Nation," that is, intermarried whites, and permitted them to establish a turnpike company with the authority to charge tolls in order to maintain the road. "Mixed blood" James Vann won the right to operate the ferry over the Chattahoochee as well as a contract to carry the mail.[91] In 1805 Alexander Cornells and William McIntosh supported the construction of the Federal Road through the Creek Nation in anticipation of opening taverns and operating ferries.[92] The Choctaws Greenwood LeFlore and David Folsom owned taverns.[93] George Colbert, a prominent Chickasaw, operated a ferry at Mussel Shoals where the Natchez Trace crossed the Tennessee River, and his brothers Levi and James owned taverns in the Chickasaw Nation along the Natchez Trace that linked Nashville with the Mississippi River.[94]

Herding livestock and operating taverns and ferries permitted both "mixed bloods" and "full-bloods" to become wealthy in enterprises that did not seriously compromise fundamental practices. The economy of "civilization," however, rested on commercial agriculture, which challenged southeastern Indians' division of labor and construction of gender. Southern Indians had been farming for over four thousand years when Hawkins arrived, so the concept of agriculture was not new to them. But their agriculture differed in major ways from the kind of farming policy-makers envisioned. First of all, women farmed; men hunted and traded. These gender roles extended far beyond a mere division of labor. In Cherokee society, for example, the first woman was Selu, the word Cherokees use for corn and the corn spirit. Being a woman was intrinsically linked to growing corn, and southern Indians essentially reclassified men who farmed rather than hunted as women.[95] Perhaps because they had adopted the gender conventions of their hosts or because they did not have the right to land, few intermarried white men farmed. As a result, virtually no examples of "civilized" farming existed within southern Indian society in the 1790s. Hawkins tried to remedy the situation by setting up a model plantation, and while his blacksmiths and millers found a following, he initially encountered little enthusiasm for Anglo-American-style farming.[96] As long as trade in commodities ranging from deerskins to stolen horses and slaves offered a good return, few men expressed much interest in agriculture. In the first decade of the nineteenth century, however, commercial opportunities began to wane, and Indians with white ancestry and those without began to invest in agriculture.

Commercial agriculture promised substantial profits for those who had capital to invest, particularly since the tribes held land in common and permitted any tribal citizen to clear and cultivate as much land as he or she wished without infringing on the rights of others. By 1801 Hawkins could boast that "the Chickasaws are settling out from their old towns and fencing their farms. . . . All of these farmers have cattle or hogs and some of the men attend seriously to labour." Other tribes were making similar progress. In 1801 Hawkins cited George Colbert, a "mixed blood" who served as the Chickasaw speaker, as "an example that has stimulated others." Hawkins's praise is revealing. Colbert, according to Hawkins, "ha[d] laboured at the plough and hoe during the last season," an acknowledgment that the speaker had not farmed previously. But Hawkins grossly exaggerated the Chickasaw headman's role since Colbert's African American slaves almost certainly performed the actual labor of farming.

The use of slave labor (and, to a far more limited extent, white sharecroppers) enabled Indian entrepreneurs to engage in commercial farming without actually doing the farming themselves.

In 1836, Albert Gallatin cynically calculated that "the number of plows in the five tribes answered for the number of able bodied negroes."[97] The absence of a uniform census makes the slave population among the southern Indians before 1860 difficult to calculate, but the rolls compiled in preparation for their removal west of the Mississippi provide some indication of the extent of slaveholding. In 1830 there were 512 slaves among the Choctaws. The large slaveholders descended from whites—Greenwood LeFlore with thirty-two slaves, his brothers with sixteen, David Folsom with ten, Joseph and James Perry with fifty-one, and Delilah Brashears with sixteen. But other Choctaws with no white ancestry also owned slaves—Mushulatubbee owned ten—and they made up the bulk of small slaveholders.[98] Among the Cherokees, as historians William G. McLoughlin and Walter H. Conser Jr., have demonstrated statistically, "mixed blood" families were far more likely to own slaves than "full-blood" ones, but a number of "full-bloods" did have slaves, including the prominent warrior and headman Major Ridge, who owned fifteen.[99] Most of the 255 slaveholders among the Chickasaws were also "mixed blood," but some "full-bloods" also owned slaves, whose number totaled 1,223 in 1839.[100] The same pattern holds for the Creeks, who in 1832 owned 902 slaves.[101] Slave labor enabled "mixed blood" entrepreneurs to conform to the gender conventions of their mothers' people by relieving them of the necessity of farming themselves. Consequently, they could be "both white and red."

Slavery, like many other aspects of early-nineteenth-century Native life, was an innovation, and headmen took new measures to protect their investment in slaves and other forms of private property. In 1808, the Cherokees established a national police force "to suppress horse stealing and robbery of other property."[102] By 1830, the Chickasaws, Choctaws, and Creeks had all passed laws that gave national protection to individual property. No longer did a person turn to a maternal uncle to recover stolen horses; the national government assumed responsibility.[103] The creation of centralized governments with coercive powers was a major innovation. Not everyone within the Indian nations agreed with the scope of change, particularly when national governments began to overshadow decision-making based in traditional towns and divisions. "Mixed bloods" usually were in the forefront of change, both because they had, on average, more property to protect and because they had a disproportionate share of political power. Once again, however, a simple racial dichotomy does not accurately reflect the political innovations or the opposition. In the Creek Nation, for example, many of those who had grievances against the national council were "mixed bloods" from lower Creek towns who thought that their views were not adequately represented.[104]

While the protection of private property certainly provided an impetus for strengthening national governments, an even stronger motivation, one that served to quiet most opposition, was the growing threat to tribal sovereignty. In the 1820s, an increasing number of politicians demanded that the United States abandon its practice of making treaties with Indians and simply deport the eastern tribes to new homelands west of the Mississippi. Although the federal government, even under the leadership of Andrew Jackson, never acceded to these demands, the rhetoric seriously undermined the process of treaty-making, and the appointment of unscrupulous political lackeys as agents and treaty commissioners increased the danger that they might force or bribe unauthorized factions to cede land. The southern Indians' national councils passed laws that prohibited land cessions and made death the penalty for violations. The execution of William McIntosh in 1825 for selling the Creeks' Georgia lands dispelled any doubt that the Indians' centralized tribal governments possessed the will to act.[105]

Perhaps more than anything else, the determination of national leaders to preserve their nations demonstrates the fallacy of characterizing "mixed bloods" as different from other Indians in the Southeast. "Mixed bloods" as well as "full-bloods" understood the deep bond between their people and the land on which they lived in the Southeast. Stories explained how each tribe came to live in a particular place. The Cherokees lived in the center of an island whose earth had been sculpted into mountains and valleys by a primordial buzzard.[106] The Chickasaws wandered widely until the sacred bent pole which they carried on their migrations to direct their course stood erect.[107] The Choctaws emerged out of the Nanih Waiya, a mound in Mississippi.[108] The Creeks, like the Chickasaws whom they included in their creation story, moved steadily toward the sunrise, constantly fighting enemies, until they reached the Chattahoochee and decided to live in peace.[109] Returning west meant encountering old enemies and certain death. The sophisticated planters who led the Cherokees, Chickasaws, Choctaws, and Creeks in the 1820s had not forgotten the essence of these myths. When the Cherokees wrote their constitution in 1827, a document usually described as a replica of those of the states, they included a uniquely Cherokee feature in Article 1: they carefully delineated the boundaries of their nation, the land meant for them. Their government, constitutional though it might be, was as intrinsically linked to place as that of their ancestors, both mythical and real. Furthermore, it affirmed that the lands were the "common property of the Nation." That is, no individual, however wealthy or powerful, owned the soil itself, nor could he sell it.[110] The Native elite benefited personally from common landholding because they did not have to invest capital in land, but their commitment ran far deeper than personal interest.

In the end, however, the struggle of southern Indians to preserve their nations in the east failed, not so much because of the lack of unity and resolve on the part of the Indians but because of the overwhelming power of the United States. The Choctaws signed a removal treaty in 1830, and the Creeks and Chickasaws followed suit in 1832. An unauthorized faction negotiated Cherokee removal in 1835. Seminoles, objecting to what they claimed was a fraudulent treaty in 1832, launched an armed resistance that lasted until 1842, when the United States declared victory and left a handful of people in the Everglades of south Florida.[111] In the wake of treaties, a few "mixed bloods" decided to remain in the east. Choctaw Greenwood LeFlore, who signed the Choctaw removal treaty, went on to an illustrious career in Mississippi politics.[112] Many of the descendants of William Weatherford, Red Stick leader and nephew of Alexander McGillivray, remained in Alabama.[113] William Rogers, who signed the Cherokee removal treaty, did not go west. He continued to live in Georgia, which in 1838 extended citizenship rights to twenty-two "mixed blood" families, including his.[114] But the vast majority of "mixed bloods" went west, sharing the ordeal of the trail of tears with their kin. Cherokee principal chief John Ross, whom historians often gratuitously note was seven-eighths white and spoke Cherokee imperfectly, lost his wife in a tragedy that, whatever his ancestry, made him undeniably Cherokee.[115]

When Oconostota proposed giving Alexander Cameron's son a piece of Cherokee land, he acknowledged the son as a Cherokee even though he had a white father. His Cherokee mother and the clan ties he inherited from her made him a Cherokee, and the grant of land confirmed and reinforced that identity. By the nineteenth century, many southern Indians were, like Cameron's son, "both white and red" in terms of ancestry and culture. In our accounts of them, however, the white often obscures the red. We are blinded by the spectacle of Indians living in mansions, owning plantations and African American slaves, sending their children to school, worshipping in Christian churches, governing themselves under constitutions and written laws. In our analysis of "mixed blood" Indians, we have privileged whiteness, and as a result, we have underestimated the power and persistence of the culture into which they were born and chose to live. By looking for the "red" in those who came to dominate the governments and economies of southern Indians in the early nineteenth century, perhaps we can better understand their societies and the ways in which they coped with the challenges of white racism.

CHAPTER THREE

"Designing Half-Breeds"

The Politics of Race

In 1816, as he tried to negotiate a land cession with the Chickasaws, Andrew Jackson fumed that the resistance he encountered came from "the designing half-breeds and renegade white men who have taken refuge in the country."[1] Like many whites of his generation, Jackson regarded Indians as simple and naïve, almost childlike. He did not believe that they could mount the kind of opposition that he had confronted. Consequently, their refusal to do his bidding meant that someone else was manipulating them, in this case, "half-breeds and renegade white men." Jackson implied that the behavior of these men—their resistance to his demands— correlated to their ancestry and that people of European descent acted differently than Indians. Jackson not only linked behavior to race, but he also made race a signifier of power: Indians needed to be led by Europeans. "Half-breeds and renegade white men" held political authority over "real Indians," whom he defined as the "natives of the forest." That these defiant men simply might be representing the views of "real Indians" was unthinkable. Racial designations, therefore, became more than descriptors; white politicians invested them with political meanings that came to have important implications for Indians and non-Indians, that is, for the South as a whole.

When Andrew Jackson ascribed certain characteristics to "half-breeds," he stood on the cusp of changing attitudes about race. A generation earlier, few people would have accepted the notion of an intrinsic link between race and behavior. Instead, Europeans had a long intellectual tradition that supported the unity of humankind and their fundamental equality, ideas embodied in the Declaration of Independence and countless other documents stretching back for centuries. In the sixteenth century, the Spanish Bishop Bartolomé de las Casas had convinced his sovereign that Indians had souls and, therefore, were human beings. Other Europeans accepted this view and, when they came to the Americas, at least gave lip service to the goal of Christianizing the Indians. Among English colonists, only New England Puritans made any substantial effort to convert Indians—and they quickly lost interest—but even the most irreligious seventeenth-century Englishman usually described Native people and cultures as "heathen," the opposite of "Christian," and attributed what they perceived as deviant behavior to Satan. With conversion, most believed, Indians would leave their heathen ways, as well as beliefs, behind them.[2] In the eighteenth century, more secular explanations of human difference emerged, and like many ideas of the Enlightenment, these enjoyed considerable popularity in the British colonies. Most Enlightenment thinkers concurred that difference stemmed from environment and education rather than inherent capabilities.[3] Virginia planter William Byrd, for example, wrote in 1728 that "All Nations of men have the same Natural Dignity, and we all know that very bright Talents may be lodg'd under a very dark Skin. The principal Difference between one People and another proceeds only from the different Opportunities of Improvement."[4] Thomas Jefferson asserted in his *Notes on the State of Virginia* that Indians "are formed in mind as well as in body, on the same module with the 'Homo sapiens Europaenus.' " He assured a correspondent that "proofs of genius given by the Indians of North America, place them on a level with Whites in the same uncultivated state."[5] As different as Catholic, Puritan, and Enlightenment views were, all rested on the assumption that human beings had a common origin, that they had souls and/or reason, and that they had the capacity to change the way they lived.

Europeans in the eighteenth century were even less clear than we are today about which characteristics individuals inherit and which they acquire, so the extent to which they thought human beings could change sometimes strikes us as preposterous. Many people, for example, believed that skin color was the product of the environment and emollients, that is, behavior rather than genetics.[6] Virginian Robert Beverley maintained that the skin of Native infants was "much clearer" than that of adults, who acquired a darker hue by "greasing and sunning themselves."[7] By refraining from these practices, Native Americans presumably could become white. And if skin color, the physical feature at which Europeans most often recoiled, was artificial, what was to prevent the transformation of Indians in other ways and, ultimately, their incorporation into colonial society?

Physical as well as cultural assimilation was both possible and desirable, according to many Euro-Americans, and the easiest means to accomplish assimilation was intermarriage.[8] John Rolfe, a prosperous and pious Virginian, became the model for this method of incorporating Indians when he married Pocahontas in 1614, several years after she supposedly saved John Smith. A year before her marriage to Rolfe, colonial authorities had taken the eighteen-year-old Pocahontas hostage, separating her from her Indian husband and her father, the region's paramount chief, whom colonists hoped to pressure into peace by holding his daughter. At the end of a year's captivity, Pocahontas converted to Christianity, took the name Rebecca, and married Rolfe. Two years later, she and her new husband, along with their infant son, traveled to England, where Pocahontas charmed the king and London society. She then died, just before her return to Virginia. The only portrait done during her lifetime depicts her as a proper Jacobean lady, not an Indian princess, and her son and his descendants ethnically identified as white even as they boasted descent from Pocahontas.[9]

In 1705 Robert Beverley lamented the failure of most Englishmen to follow Rolfe's example and marry Indians. Had they done so, he believed, there would have been far less bloodshed in Virginia, which had been wracked by Indian wars in its first four decades, and the population would have increased rapidly as a result of lives spared, children conceived, and English immigration expanded.[10] Two decades later, William Byrd proposed "that there is but one way of converting these poor Infidels, and reclaiming them from Barbarity, and that is to Charitably intermarry with them."[11] Subsequent writers also advocated intermarriage. Edmund Atkin, who prepared a report on colonial Indian affairs in 1755, thought it "prudent to encourage" marriage between soldiers garrisoned on the frontier and Indian women "by which means our Interest among the Indians will be strengthened." He even suggested transporting to the frontier "able bodied men *Convicts* of petty crimes, instead of being hanged, or incorporated among the People of our Colonies." There they would plant corn for the Indians, marry Indian women, receive an allotment of land, and in Atkin's words, "strengthen the place."[12] Beverley and Atkin were not alone in advocating intermarriage for diplomatic and strategic purposes. The Spanish governor of West Florida, Arturo O'Neill, proposed intermarriage as a way to bind the Creeks to Spain because, as he asserted, "mestizo sons . . . are most inclined toward the whites."[13]

Early United States Indian policy sought to assimilate Indians for their own good. Thomas Jefferson wrote Benjamin Hawkins, the United States agent to the Creeks, that "the ultimate point of rest and happiness for them is to let our settlements and theirs meet and blend together, to intermix, and become one people."[14] Jefferson, however, did not anticipate a homogenized society in which cultures blended together and produced a new way of thinking and behaving. Enlightenment thinkers established a hierarchy of human cultures with hunters and gatherers on the bottom, pastoralists a bit higher, subsistence agriculturalists still higher, and their own exalted "civilized" culture at the top. Societies that appeared less complex, like those of the Indians, presumably could not survive in close proximity to more sophisticated ones. Instead of using their disparate traditions to create a new society, many eighteenth-century Anglo-Americans sought to extinguish Native cultures and individually absorb Indians into their community, just as they had transformed Pocahontas into the Christian English-woman, Rebecca. Jefferson expressed his view of the inevitability of this process in his letter to Hawkins: "Incorporating themselves with us as citizens of the United States, this is what the natural progress of things will, of course, bring on."[15] Policy-makers like Jefferson saw this obliteration of Native cultures as fundamentally benevolent because they believed that these cultures and the people who clung to them were doomed unless they abandoned their "savage" ways and became "civilized."

The belief in the ability of Indians to change and the certainty of their destruction if they did not gave rise to the United States' "civilization" program, which tried to change Indians culturally by teaching them plow agriculture, spinning and weaving, animal husbandry, republican government, the English language, and Christian religious beliefs. The architects of the "civilization" policy believed that the previous failures of Indians to achieve "civilization" on their own resulted from their lack of knowledge and that, with proper training, they could become culturally indistinguishable from their non-Indian neighbors. It never occurred to policy-makers that Indians could not accomplish this goal because of some inherent inferiority or because they might choose to retain their own cultures and beliefs. Advocates of "civilization" were confident that, with education, Indians would recognize instantly the fundamental superiority of Anglo-American culture and abandon their own ways of life for it.

Evangelical Protestants, convinced that "civilization or extinction must be the lot of all the Indian tribes within our borders," embraced the effort in force after the War of 1812 and established missions among the southern Indians.[16] "It is very natural for these people," missionaries wrote of the Choctaws, "either from their good sense, or from the principle of imitation, to fall in with the customs of their more civilized neighbors."[17] When white neighbors did not provide very good examples, missionaries seized the opportunity to demonstrate the Indians' ability to change and to justify their own evangelical work. Missionary Ard Hoyt "found a striking and affecting contrast between two families [he] visited." The children of the "mixed blood" Cherokee family were "instructed in letters and religion;—acquainted with family prayer;—decent and orderly in all family duties;—christianized and civilized." On the other hand, the children of a white family who lived on the border of the Cherokee Nation were "totally ignorant of letters, and of religion;—not one of them could tell who made them, who made the world, or who is the Savior;—unchristianized and sinking into the savage state, if not already there."[18] Behavior not ancestry, therefore, defined "savagery," and missionaries joined with the United States government to banish "savagery" among southern Indians.

Embracing William Byrd's notion that "a sprightly Lover is the most prevailing Missionary," early United States policy encouraged intermarriage.[19] Benjamin Hawkins came to the Creeks in

1796 "in favour of the idea of forming amorous connexions with the women, [and] had in contemplation to set the example myself and order my assistants to follow." Interracial couples living at the agency, he anticipated, would set a "civilized" standard to which other Creeks would aspire. This plan came to a screeching halt, however, when the agency blacksmith's Creek wife took command of his house and belongings and generously shared everything she controlled with her large, extended family.[20] Hawkins promptly prohibited further intermarriage. The Cherokee agent, Return J. Meigs, was more optimistic. In 1808 he defended his position favoring such unions to two headmen who feared that intermarried white men would compromise the Cherokees' claim to their land: "You say I encouraged marriages between white men & Cherokee women. I always have and shall do it because your women are industrious & because I conceive that by this measure civilization is farther advanced than in any other way having always considered the whole human race as brothers."[21] Both Meigs and Hawkins believed that intermarriage aided the "civilization" program because intermarried whites could teach first their spouses about "civilized" life and then serve as an example to other Indians.

The failure of Hawkins's original scheme for promoting "civilization" through intermarriage points to a serious flaw in the Enlightenment's conception of culture—people of supposedly "lower" cultures did not automatically adopt the practices of "higher" cultures; in fact, they often resisted giving up their own cultural traditions. In the late eighteenth century, Bernard Romans noted that the Indians "would think themselves degraded in the lowest degree, were they to imitate us in any respect whatever, and . . . look down on us and all our manners with the highest contempt."[22] In other words, many Indians preferred their own ways of doing things.

Native people had an explanation for why they were reluctant to adopt the white man's ways. In rejecting the schools that an 1823 treaty provided for the Seminoles, Neamathla told the governor of Florida, "We wish our children to remain as the Great Spirit made them, and as their fathers are, Indians. . . . If you establish a school, and teach our people the knowledge of the white people, they will cease to be Indians." He then explained that after the Master of Life created the world, he decided to make a man. His first attempt turned out white. The Great Spirit, according to Neamathla, "was sorry: he saw that the being he had made was pale and weak; he took pity on him, and therefore did not unmake him, but let him live." His next effort turned out black, "and he shoved him aside to make room for another trial. Then it was that he made the *red man;* and the red man pleased him." The Great Spirit gave each man a choice of one of three boxes that contained tools. The white man, whom the Great Spirit pitied, chose first, and he took the box containing pens, paper, compasses, and other things that white people use. The Great Spirit pushed the black man aside and let the red man choose next because, he said, "the red man is my favorite." The red man "chose a box filled with tomahawks, knives, war-clubs, traps, and such things that are useful in war and hunting." The black man was left with a box of "axes and hoes, with buckets to carry water in, and long whips for driving oxen, which meant," according to Neamathla, "that the negro must work for both the red and white man, and it has been so ever since." Thomas McKenney, who administered United States Indian policy between 1816 and 1830, recorded Neamathla's account and characterized it as "of his own invention," but other Southeastern peoples had similar explanations for the three races: they had separate origins and purposes.[23] These accounts originated after Europeans and Africans arrived in the Americas and reflected colonial race relations. Nevertheless, they expressed how many nineteenth-century Native southerners viewed their role in the world and explained why they were reluctant to jeopardize their place as the Great Spirit's favorite. This conception of race and culture, needless to say, clearly contradicted the philosophy underlying the United States' "civilization" program.

The response of Native people to "civilization" varied by tribes and individuals, but the pattern is remarkably similar. People adopted aspects of "civilization" that seemed useful to them and avoided practices that challenged deeply held values and beliefs. Men, for example, took up livestock herding, but in many ways they had simply restocked the forests, which had been heavily depleted of game, with cattle and hogs. Leaving animals to forage in the woods meant that men had to round them up for sale, an activity that lasted for much of the fall, the traditional season for hunting. The similarities between the two activities are reflected in the Cherokee Doublehead's choice of words, used to explain why he delayed a trip: "I am so engaged in hunting and gathering my beef cattle that I expect it will be a moon or two before I can come."[24] Women continued to do much of the farming in most families, according to the traditional division of labor, with men helping only in soil preparation and harvest. Wealthy men who wanted to expand their agricultural production engaged white sharecroppers or purchased African slaves; they did not farm themselves. Familial arrangements changed somewhat as some men, many of them of European ancestry, cleared plantations and built substantial houses separate from traditional towns. Even these households, however, often centered around female kin since prominent men frequently married sisters and lived in polygamous families in which everyone was related under matrilineal kinship rules—everyone except for them. Cherokees, Chickasaws, Choctaws, and Creeks also passed law codes in the decades before removal that centralized authority, but customary law continued to function and, in some cases, such as the matrilineal descent of property, came to incorporate traditional practice.[25] And while missionaries made important strides in converting southern Indians to Christianity among the Cherokees,

Chickasaws, and Choctaws, only about 10 percent of the Cherokees ever joined the church, and perhaps half of these ended up expelled.[26] The genuineness of Chickasaw and Choctaw conversions also is questionable because when they realized that the acceptance of "civilization," including Christianity, was not going to prevent their removal to the West, they left Christian churches in droves.[27] Indians accepted change when it made sense to them—shifting from hunting to commercial agriculture, for example, and learning to speak English—but most saw little reason to abandon fulfilling practices and beliefs for those of Anglo-Americans.

As years passed, the uneven progress of "civilization" among the Indians became a growing concern, especially since objectives far less altruistic than saving the Indians from certain destruction also motivated policy-makers. As the population of the United States grew in the decades following the American Revolution, politicians sought to make more land available to its citizens. Converting Indian hunters into Indian farmers, a goal of the "civilization" program, promised to free thousands of acres of "hunting grounds" for white purchase and settlement. To this end, Thomas Jefferson instructed Benjamin Hawkins in 1803 "to promote among the Indians a sense of the superior value of a little land, well cultivated, over a great deal, unimproved." Eventually, he anticipated, their hunting grounds east of the Mississippi "will be found useless, and even disadvantageous."[28] Those Indians who wanted to continue hunting could exchange their share of tribal lands for tracts west of the Mississippi where game was more plentiful; those who remained in their homeland could farm on their reduced but still adequate land base and become assimilated into American culture. Even as game declined in the late eighteenth and early nineteenth centuries, however, Indians proved remarkably unwilling to part with the depleted hunting grounds that most whites considered to be "surplus & waste lands."[29] A chorus of politicians echoed the sentiments of Cherokee agent Return J. Meigs, who complained that these lands served only as "a nursery of savage habits and operates against civilization," but no one in Jefferson's era officially advocated forcing them to surrender title. Native people, after all, had the same natural rights as Euro-Americans since they were all one people with a common origin and equal potential.[30]

Attitudes about human difference, however, were changing.[31] In the early nineteenth century, intellectuals increasingly questioned the fundamental equality of humankind and suggested that immutable differences unalterably divided peoples. Even in the eighteenth century, a vocal minority, including the esteemed French philosopher Voltaire, had insisted that differences in human cultures and appearances derived from separate origins that produced distinct species of people. Bernard Romans, a late-eighteenth-century naturalist who traveled among Indians of the lower South, firmly believed "that God created an original man and woman in this part of the globe, of a different species from any in the other parts." As a separate species, the Indians were "a people not only rude and uncultivated, but incapable of civilization."[32]

Such radical views of separate origins would not find formal acceptance in the United States until the middle of the nineteenth century. Long before then, a new intellectual movement called Romanticism, which ultimately overwhelmed the rationalist ideas of the Enlightenment, had raised doubts about the success of culturally changing Indians. In addition to its artistic, literary, and musical manifestations, Romanticism stressed the uniqueness of national identities, a concept that legitimized the nineteenth-century configuration of European states and emboldened Americans to declare cultural independence from Europe. More perniciously, Romanticism linked culture and race. Each people had unique qualities that were inherent and immutable, and these qualities extended beyond merely physical characteristics such as skin and hair color. Political and economic structures, artistic expressions and sensibilities, even moral and ethical standards were the exclusive product of a particular race of people and could not be transferred to another. This belief called into question the United States' program for "civilizing" Indians and gave rise to the adage, "Once an Indian, always an Indian."

Many Americans, especially those who lived west of the Appalachians, had long taken issue with the Enlightenment view of Indians that emanated from Europe and the eastern United States, but racial antipathy to Indians mounted in the early nineteenth century. Immediately preceding the War of 1812, an Indian confederacy in the Old Northwest had militarily resisted United States expansion, and in the Southeast, the Creek civil war of 1813 claimed white lives and property. The Panic of 1819, which many southerners believed could have been mitigated by more easily available land—Indian land—only exacerbated tension. Clamor arose to divest Indians of their landholdings and move them west of the Mississippi. Some Choctaws and Cherokees had, in fact, moved west permanently in the first two decades of the nineteenth century, and other Indians crossed the Mississippi on hunting expeditions. These migrations were voluntary and limited, fulfilling the Jeffersonian vision of the west as a place for Indians who wanted to continue their traditional way of life, presumably by hunting. In the 1820s, however, Jefferson's plan, which had expected the assimilation of those Indians who remained in the East, succumbed to racism, fanned by white population growth, economic uncertainty, and political demagoguery. White southerners demanded relegating Indians still living in the southern states to an inferior social and legal status or, preferably, forcing them to Indian territory west of the Mississippi.

Southern Indians refused to consider selling their lands in the east and moving west. The overwhelming majority of all tribes shared the sentiments of a group of Cherokee women who reminded their national council in 1818 that "The land was given to us by the Great Spirit above as our common right, to raise our children upon, & to make support for our rising generations."[33] They had no intention of leaving. Furthermore, the opposition to removal was almost universal. The American Board of Commissioners for Foreign Missions reported in 1830 that "respecting the Cherokees, Chickasaws, and Choctaws [among whom they had missionaries], it is uniformly to this effect, that these tribes, almost to a man, wish to remain in the lands of their fathers, and that there is no topic of so much general interest and on which the Indians feel so much anxiety and distress than that of their apprehended removal."[34] In the face of such united opposition, proponents of removal had to discredit Native rights to the land and the Indians' insistence that they did not want to move.

The image of Indians that dominated public rhetoric in the decades following the War of 1812 portrayed them as "sons of the forest." Northern Indians, who depended more heavily on hunting, fishing, and gathering than southern Indians and often migrated in a seasonal cycle, shaped this view, but since it served important political purposes in the South, the image gained wide currency. Ignoring the fact that southern Indians had been living in permanent villages and cultivating the soil for thousands of years, politicians depicted them as leading a "wandering life."[35] Their purported failure to farm presumably invalidated their title to vast landholdings in the South, land which white farmers could transform from wilderness to plantations. For that reason, Georgia congressman Wilson Lumpkin appealed to his colleagues to deny "Indian claims to large tracts of country on which they have neither dwelt nor made improvements, merely because they have seen them from the mountain or passed them in the chase."[36] Efforts to "civilize" the Indians and convert them into yeoman farmers, according to Lumpkin, had largely failed, and most "retained their savage habits."[37]

Indians did not forsake their "savage habits," many politicians contended, because they could not. Lewis Cass, who had served for eighteen years as the governor of Michigan Territory and ultimately became Jackson's secretary of war, made the most persuasive case for the inability of Indians to change: "Distress could not teach them providence, nor want industry. As animal food decreased, their vegetable productions were not increased. Their habits were stationary and unbending; never changing with the change of cir cumstances. . . . There is a principle of repulsion in ceaseless ac- tivity, operating through all their institutions, which prevents them from appreciating or adopting any other modes of life, or any other habits of thought or action, but those which have descended to them from their ancestors."[38] The Indians had not changed because "savagery" was an inborn trait; "civilization" was impossible for them, so they could never establish legitimate title to their home- lands in the Southeast.

The views of Lumpkin, Cass, and other politicians extended far beyond the halls of Congress. Popular writers seized upon the re- lations between Indians and whites as an appropriate subject for their fiction. Some, such as James Fenimore Cooper in *The Last of the Mohicans,* published in 1826, portrayed Indians in a sympathetic light, perpetuating a "noble savage" trope, but however "noble" the Indians in his fiction might be, they were still "savages" doomed to extinction. In *The Yemassee: A Romance of Carolina,* published in 1835, South Carolinian William Gilmore Simms conceded the for- mer nobility of the Yamassee Indians, but the whites who lived around them had corrupted them. Unable to become "civilized," they lost their nobility and remained merely "savages." In both Cooper's and Simms's work, according to literary scholar Dana

Nelson, Native individuality declined as the novels progressed, and Indians merged into a mob that was a "dangerous and degraded force." This characterization served to set them apart from whites and to reinforce racial as well as national consciousness.[39]

The arguments for dispossessing the Indians also found support in the scientific community. In particular, phrenology, whose practitioners analyzed skulls in order to ascertain intelligence and character, imparted scientific respectability to political and literary views. By analyzing a large number of skulls from a particular race, phrenologists expanded their analysis from individuals to entire categories of human beings and developed racial rankings that, not surprisingly, put whites on top. George Combe, a Scot who had great influence on the development of phrenology in the United States, concluded that "the existing races of native American Indians show skulls inferior in the moral and intellectual development to those of the Anglo-Saxon race." This inherent inferiority explained the Indians' declining population and influence in the United States: "morally and intellectually, these Indians are inferior to their Anglo-Saxon invaders, and have receded before them."[40] Phrenologists also flatly denied the possibility of "civilizing" Indians. Dr. Charles Caldwell, one of this country's most acclaimed practitioners and a proponent of the view that Indians and Europeans were separate species, examined the heads of a number of Indians and concluded that "when the wolf, the buffalo and the panther shall have been completely domesticated, . . . then, and not before, may we expect to see the *full-blooded* Indian civilized, like the white man."[41]

Even some people who had long promoted "civilization" began to have doubts about the ability of Indians to be assimilated into American culture. Among them was Thomas McKenney, the head of the Office of Indian Affairs, who encountered overt discrimination at an inn just outside Augusta when he entered with two Creek boys whom he was taking to Washington to receive an education. Although the boys had bathed, cut their long hair, and donned new suits, the proprietress sprang to her feet, clenched her fist, and announced to McKenney, "Sir, I will not allow Indians to come to my table." McKenney insisted that the boys be fed, and so she summoned her husband who repeated the admonition. McKenney responded, "Those little boys are very near to me, and I shall see, wherever I go, that they occupy the same level which I do." Cowed by McKenney, the man departed the room in a huff, and the party finished breakfast.[42] When McKenney left office in 1830, the Creek boys remained in Washington and later returned to their people. At the time McKenney wrote his memoirs in the 1840s, he had heard nothing further about the younger boy, but the older one had come to no good. He got into a murderous brawl, fled to Florida, and joined the Seminoles in their armed struggle against removal. Despite the advantage of a Washington education, in even the sympathetic McKenney's account, he reverted to "savagery." Though less visceral than the racial hostility the boys had endured at the Augusta inn, McKenney's characterization of their fate was as degrading.

The increasingly virulent racism of white Americans began to pose problems for those who wanted to marry across racial lines. The most notorious incident involving intermarriage occurred in the mid-1820s when Cherokee cousins John Ridge and Elias Boudinot married New England women whom they had met while attending school in Cornwall, Connecticut. The editor of the *American Eagle,* published in Litchfield, Connecticut, characterized the Ridge nuptials as an "unnatural connection," and the board of the Foreign Mission School, where the two Cherokees were students, branded Boudinot's courtship as "criminal." Despite the board's condemnation of intermarriage, public outcry forced the school to close its doors in the wake of the second marriage.[43] The marriages of

Ridge and Boudinot to white women forced racism into the open in reputedly tolerant and pious New England and made overt racial hostility an acceptable part of public discourse. Shutting down the Foreign Mission School marked a surrender of evangelicalism to these new views of Indians and their role in American society.

The growing conviction that Indians were unable to change not only called into question the positive influence of intermarried whites but also raised questions about the capabilities and proclivities of their "mixed blood" offspring. Until race began to dominate scientific investigation of human difference, mixed race people, even those of African and European descent, commanded little attention.[44] In 1811 the esteemed scholar, Dr. Benjamin Rush, suggested that "mixed race" children represented an improvement over either of their parents: "The mulatto has been remarked, in all countries, to exceed, in sagacity, his white and black parent. The same remark has been made of the offspring of the European, and the North American Indian."[45] By the 1820s, scientists tended to presume that these children had intelligence superior to the Native parent but inferior to the European. Nevertheless, the children were thought to possess a greater affinity for European culture than that of the Natives because they recognized its inherent superiority. Whatever hope remained for "civilizing" Indians was limited to those of mixed blood, and the phrenologist Dr. Charles Caldwell argued that "the only efficient scheme to civilize the Indians is to *cross the breed*."[46] Whites began to see "mixed blood" as a specific category with its own inherent characteristics distinct from those of either parent. The same intellectual process took place for the descendants of Europeans and Africans, and by 1850 the category "mulatto" had become so significant in the American mind that the United States census began enumerating these individuals separately. In the era of Indian removal, therefore, new categories entered the racial hierarchy that now ranked "mixed blood" Indians above "full-bloods" but below whites.

A category of "mixed blood" Indian served an important purpose in the emerging racial ideology, especially since many southern Indians had taken up commercial agriculture, republican political institutions, Anglo-American dress and manners, the English language, and even Christianity. These "civilized" Indians seemed to belie the emerging conventional wisdom about racial difference. How could the new racial conviction that non-whites were intrinsically inferior square with the reality that some people of Native descent had become "civilized"? One possible explanation for this discrepancy was that successes were limited to "mixed blood" Indians, who presumably stood somewhere between the two races that gave birth to them. Certainly, "mixed bloods" had come to play a prominent role in the economic systems and governments of southeastern Indians in the early nineteenth century. Now observers began to focus attention on them as "mixed bloods," attribute their behavior to their ancestry, and characterize them as more "progressive" and more "civilized" than Indians who had no white ancestry.

The Cherokees attracted the most attention because they established a constitutional government in 1827 and a bilingual newspaper in 1828. Georgia congressman Wilson Lumpkin admitted in 1830 that "we do find in the Cherokee country many families enjoying all the common comforts of civil and domestic life, and possessing the necessary means to secure these enjoyments." The Cherokees also had schools and churches, but "the principle part of these enjoyments are confined to the blood of the white man, either in whole or in part." According to Lumpkin, "a large portion of the full-blooded Cherokees still remain a poor degraded race of human beings." Imposing his own assumptions about class,

Lumpkin held United States Indian policy responsible for "furnish-
ing the means to create the Cherokee aristocracy." While the "real
Indians" lived in abject poverty, their "lords and rulers [who] are
white men, and descendants of white men, [were] enjoying the fat
of the land, and enjoying exclusively the Government annuities."[47]
Lewis Cass conceded "that individuals among the Cherokees have
acquired property, and with it more enlarged views and juster notions of the value of our institutions, and the unprofitableness of
their own . . . [but] this change of opinion and condition is confined, in a great measure, to some of the *half-breeds* and their im-
mediate connexions."[48]

The subtle shift in attitudes is evident even in the work of evangelical missionaries, who showed an increasing tendency to use
race to categorize Native people. Representatives of the American
Board of Commissioners for Foreign Missions, the most successful evangelical organization among southern Indians, ostensibly
grounded their work in Enlightenment assumptions about human
equality and potential. As one missionary wrote in 1822, "Civilization, and a knowledge of the Scriptures will, doubtless, dispel
the mist which has so long hung over these nations, and show
them to be not inferior to any other people."[49] Nevertheless, in re-
ports of their converts, the children in their schools, and the people
they met, they almost always identified them by ancestry, sometimes recording the information on church rolls in a column headed
"pedigree."[50] An account of children enrolled in the Choctaw mission at Mayhew, for example, carefully noted their "blood": "*Timothy Dickinson . . .* Full Choctaw, . . . *Edward Dwight . . .* He is of
mixed blood."[51] Upon the acceptance of two Cherokee young men
as candidates for baptism, missionaries at Brainerd commented:
"One of them is a full blooded Cherokee, could speak no English when he came, and now speaks it imperfectly. The other is a
half breed, and was taught to speak English when young." Despite

racial classification of these neophyte Christians, the missionaries affirmed their fundamental belief in equality: "They are both in the most forward class in the school, and possess considerable native strength of mind."[52]

The missionaries' constant application of racial categories to the Indian people they served, however, undermined their ideological stance on human equality. Their preference for establishing missions in neighborhoods where a majority was "mixed blood" and English-speaking also belied their pronouncements. One of their own number, Daniel Butrick, complained that most missionaries to the Cherokees focused their attention on the elite, particularly those who had some facility with English, and refused to minister to "the great body of these people."[53] Furthermore, their racial analysis of "civilization" often conformed to that of Lumpkin and Cass. American Board missionaries at Brainerd reported: "The mixed Cherokees, especially, are fast improving in their manners, and every year becoming more civilized. As a class of people, they are now quite industrious. They imitate the whites in the managing of their domestic affairs, and in the cultivation of their fields. Among the full Cherokees, also, more industrious habits are perceptible. They are now beginning to feel that the raising of corn and otherwise managing the plantation belongs to the male sex. The plough is now generally introduced, and many other farming utensils, which, for ages that are passed, they were strangers to."[54] The intent of the missionaries was to counter arguments that "civilization" extended only to a handful of "mixed bloods," but in the process, they effectively divided the Cherokee people into racial categories. Even more overtly, in their 1831 resolution condemning attempts to remove the Cherokees, missionaries contended, quite accurately, that "the Cherokees are rapidly advancing in civilization . . . as a body[;] . . . some Indians of full blood are in the foremost rank, and some of mixed blood bring up the rear." Then they asserted, "The intermixture of white people with the Indians has undoubtedly been a considerable cause of the civilization of the latter." Although they referred specifically to the example of white people and not to their "blood," missionaries' racialization of "civilization" undercut their message of universal progress and bolstered the very charges they sought to refute.[55]

Unlike their white neighbors, Native people had no category for "mixed bloods" and almost never used the term. On the rare occasions when they did, "half-breed" described or personified departures from traditional ways of doing things rather than identifying particular individuals by race. In 1801, Choctaw chief Homastubby, for example, asked Benjamin Hawkins to send women to teach them to spin and weave: "these women may go first among our half-breeds and teach them. . . . we have halfbreeds and others accustomed to work." Choctaw Robert McClure expanded the request to include a cotton gin: "We halfbreeds and young men wish to go to work."[56] Subsequent developments demonstrate that the Choctaws did not literally restrict cotton production to "half-breeds." Two decades later, cotton fields blanketed their country, Choctaw artisans had made over two thousand spinning wheels and several hundred looms, Choctaw women were producing over ten thousand yards of cloth each year, and Puckshunubbee, a "full-blood" chief, was appealing to the federal government for a gin.[57] When Levi Colbert and a group of Chickasaw headmen protested a treaty provision permitting private reservations, they distinguished between the signatories of the letter, including Colbert, his brother, and several other individuals of white ancestry, and the "halfbreeds" whom they feared "would take a great deal of the very best land and leave the poor." Colbert associated "half-breeds" with greed, and he exempted himself from that category.[58] In resisting reservations and defending common land title, Colbert was, in his own estimation, an Indian, whatever his ancestry might be. For southern Indians in the early nineteenth century, behavior defined "mixed blood," not ancestry.

Most southern Indians, whether "mixed blood" or "full-blood," expressed their identity through the clothes they wore, which were a mixture of Native and European styles and took on remarkable uniformity across the South. Most women wore long skirts, blouses, and shawls, which they often used to cover their heads, while men chose to wear a combination of European and Native clothing.[59] Their brightly colored hunting shirts, sashes, leggings, and turbans clearly identified them as Indian. In 1826 the Chickasaw agent complained that "if one of them insofar as shows a disposition to conform to them [white ways], say in dress, he is forced to abandon them or subject himself to frequent insult and his influence amongst them [is] completely destroyed."[60] Almost all the southern Indians depicted in McKenney and Hall's *The Indian Tribes of North America* wear distinctly Indian clothing. Notable exceptions include the Cherokee "full-blood" Major Ridge, who donned a white shirt, frock coat, vest, and stock, and the Choctaw "full-blood" Pushmataha, who wore his United States military uniform.[61]

The similarity in dress—and the exceptions—probably contributed to the difficulty that outsiders often had in distinguishing "full bloods" and "mixed bloods," but in addition, the eccentricity of genes created a "diversity of complexion" that made skin tone an equally imperfect determinant of ancestry. American Board missionaries noted that "some of the full Indians are so light, that, if protected from the weather as much as the people of our own country, they would not differ many shades from a dark Englishman."[62] Their descriptions of students indicate the danger in using color to determine race: "Full Choctaw, light complexion, . . . mixed blood, rather dark complexion, . . . full Choctaw, very light complexion, . . . full Choctaw, dark complexion."[63]

Names provided at least as inaccurate an indicator of ancestry as color or dress. Most southern Indians had a personal name that sometimes changed if it no longer fit the person. Men often had a public name, which was also a title. In the late eighteenth and early nineteenth centuries, many Native people took European names. Among the Creeks, for example, Alexander Cornells was also Oche Hadjo and Josiah Francis was Hillis Hadjo. The adoption of an English name did not necessarily indicate white ancestry or even personal choice. Missionaries frequently named children when they entered school, often bestowing names chosen by benefactors who paid for the privilege. The "Female Mite Society" in Baltimore, for example, contributed $18.75 "towards supporting at Brainerd [in the Cherokee Nation] the daughter of a seriously inclined Indian, to be called Caroline Smelt," and its male counterpart sent an equal sum for supporting a little boy who was to be named Nicholas Patterson.[64] Sometimes missionaries gave the same name to more than one child. A seven-year-old "full Choctaw" received the name "William Jenks" in 1824, for example, but missionaries explained that "this is the second boy, taken as a beneficiary, to whom this name has been given." The first had spent a year in the school at age twelve and then had run away. Missionaries did not comment on whether or not he continued to use the name as well. Among the "full Choctaw" classmates of William Jenks were William Goddell, Levi Parsons Oliphant, Kelso McBoyd, and Richard Salter Storrs.[65]

Just as "full-bloods" bore English names, a white father did not guarantee conformity to Anglo-American naming patterns. A white man, Hamilton Conrad, and his Cherokee wife, Onai, had three sons, Young Wolf, Rattlinggourd, and The Hair. The only son who ultimately used their white father's surname was The Hair, who became Hair Conrad in the early nineteenth century, but his children took Hair, not Conrad, as their surname. Hamilton Conrad's other grandchildren were known as Wolfs and Rattlinggourds, as are their descendants today; no descendants of Conrad bear their white progenitor's surname.[66]

Some children took their mother's surname. The descendants of Katy Grayson, daughter of a white trader and a Creek woman, and Tulwa Tustunuggee are known as Graysons. In another example, John Rogers, a Georgian who settled among the Cherokees about 1802, married Sarah Cordery, the daughter of a white man whose surname she used. The couple's first seven children were known by the surname Cordery until their father petitioned the Georgia legislature to change their name to Rogers in 1817. In the same year he received a private reservation, a tract of 640 acres on land the Cherokees ceded in what is today Gwinnett County.[67] Conrad and Grayson descendants and the Cordery-Rogers children were exceptions—children normally took their fathers' names and those names descended patrilineally—but they demonstrate that names did not always reflect race or paternity and that the exceptions occurred among "mixed bloods" as well as "full-bloods."

Native people did not use names or dress to distinguish between "mixed bloods" and "full-bloods," in part, because they saw no distinction. American Board missionaries to the Cherokees noticed that although "the intermarriages of whites and Indians have been so long practiced, that a considerable part of the tribe are of mixed blood; yet all, who are partly Indian, are spoken of as Cherokees."[68] When Cherokee Elias Boudinot, whose maternal grandfather was white, addressed audiences in New England in 1826, he asserted, "You behold here an *Indian,* my kindred are *Indians.*"[69] In his preface to a letter published in the *Missionary Herald,* the editor identified the author, David Folsom, as "a half breed Choctaw." Folsom, however, consistently referred to "we Choctaws" in the letter and closed with the words, "your unworthy red brother."[70] As late as the 1930s, the daughter of Creek chief George Washington Grayson remembered her father as a "full-blood" Creek, not because of his ancestry which, as she well knew, included a number of whites, but because he was a Creek nationalist.[71] Whatever their ancestry, Boudinot, Folsom, and even Grayson, as well as thousands of other "mixed blood" people, thought of themselves as Indians. Their behavior established their identity.

Native people did, however, view one particular group of "mixed blood" people as distinct. These were the children of Indian men and white women who had not been adopted into clans. Most white women who married Native men—a third of the whites in the Cherokee Nation in 1819, according to agent Return J. Meigs, were intermarried white women—had been captured as children, adopted into clans, and raised as Indians. From the Cherokee perspective, they were Cherokees, even though agent Meigs racially identified them as white in his census.[72] John Ridge and Elias Boudinot, however, married women who had grown up in New England. Steeped in New England evangelicalism and, like their husbands, committed to Indian "civilization," these women had no intention of conforming to Indian expectations and seeking adoption by a clan, which they regarded as a vestige of "savagery." Consequently, a number of Cherokees disapproved of the unions. John's father, Major Ridge, attributed the opposition to "the lower class of people . . . who on account of their ignorance were very much prejudiced against the white people."[73] Evidence suggests, however, that in other cases objections to intermarriage came even from people who were themselves the product of intermarriage—but intermarriages in which the maternal line was Cherokee. In the early nineteenth century, John Ross, who descended from interracial unions, "warmly opposed two such [intermarriages] in his family, and consented to a third because he believed opposition would do no good."[74] The opposition, however, was limited solely to the intermarriage of adult white women without clan ties to Cherokee men, and its basis was cultural and not racial. Without clan ties, these women and their children had no place in Cherokee society.[75]

For non-Indians increasingly concerned with racial categories, however, ancestry determined identity, and the fact that Indians did not make racial distinctions mattered little, especially when the justification for removing Indians from the Southeast shifted from a cultural argument to a racial one. Andrew Jackson, who was elected president in 1828, made Indian removal a priority.[76] During Jackson's two terms, Congress passed the Indian Removal Act that provided for the negotiation of treaties that would rid the South of Indians, all five southern tribes negotiated removal treaties, and the Choctaws and Creeks moved to their new lands in the West. Long before he became president, however, Jackson had decided that the Indians truly wanted to sell their land and go west despite considerable evidence to the contrary. As he negotiated a cession from the Chickasaws in 1816, he reported to Secretary of War William H. Crawford that "if all influence but the native Indian was out of the way, we would have but little trouble."[77] The "native Indian," in Jackson's view, had little reason to resist relocation to the West since they were merely "natives of the forest." In negotiating with the Cherokees in 1817, Jackson expressed confidence that "had the nation been left to the council of its old chiefs, we would have had but little trouble to have explained to them, their real interests, and on what their happiness and their national existance depended." Much to his dismay, however, he had to negotiate with "half-breeds, who by intrigue and corruption have got into the council of this nation and have turned out the old chiefs."[78] The real Indians appeared "to be overawed by the council of some white men and halfbreeds, who have been and are fattening upon the annuities, the labours, and folly of the native Indian, and who believe, that their income would be destroyed by the removal of the Indians."[79] The racialization of Native societies, therefore, became a tool to discredit their leadership, leadership that consistently opposed removal through the 1820s.[80]

"Mixed blood" Indians were no longer merely more "civilized" than "real Indians," they also were more immoral, dishonest, and self-serving. In making their case that "*savages cannot be civilized without Christianity,*" even American Board missionaries wrote that "the greatest effect of introducing some of the implements of civilized life, with English dress, and other things of small importance, has been to make some of the people most insatiably avaricious, leaving them as far from real civilization as before." Overwhelmingly New Englanders with anti-slavery sentiments, the missionaries referred specifically to "the half-breeds [who] have large plantations, which they cultivate by the aid of slaves."[81] Politicians, on the other hand, focused on graft and political corruption. Jackson wrote the Secretary of War from the Cherokee Agency in 1817 that "corruption . . . rules here—it flows from a few corrupt whitemen, and half breeds, who by undue means has got into the council of this nation."[82] Jackson saw parallels between these men and the "bawling politicians" in the United States, "who loudly exclaim that we are the friends of the people, but who, when the[y] obtain their views care no more for the happiness or wellfare of the people than the Devil does—but each procure influence through the same channell and for the same base purpose, *self agrandisement*."[83] He described the Cherokee government as "corrupt and Despotic" and a "self created tyranny, that is wielded by corruption to bad and unjust purposes."[84] Their subversion of democracy compounded their fiscal corruption and threatened not only their own people but also republican institutions in the United States. Congressman Lumpkin called the Cherokees' "mixed blood" leadership "the most violent and dangerous enemies of our civil institutions."[85]

The solution to this situation, for those who sought the removal of the Cherokees and other southern Indians, was the extension of state law over the Indian nations. As early as 1817, Jackson had insisted that "the laws of the u states must be extended to this country, [for] the safety of the honest here [in the Cherokee Nation] and in our neighboring states and counties." He suggested that people unwilling to submit to the laws of the state, those "who are afraid of good government," go west.[86] In 1828 Georgia extended state law over the Cherokees who lived within the chartered boundary of the state and promptly began to limit the Cherokees' civil rights. By 1830 Georgia legislation had suspended Cherokee laws and political institutions and denied Cherokees the right to testify against whites in court. Georgia severely restricted the rights of Cherokees, not because they were "savages" or "heathens," but because they were Indians. Alabama and Mississippi enacted similar legislation, and Chickasaws, Choctaws, and Creeks found themselves the victims of racial discrimination under the law. When Native leaders tried to defend their nations' sovereignty, Lumpkin interpreted the Cherokees' resistance to state action as resentment over their inability to compete with whites by citing a socially and politically prominent Virginia family: "These men, when incorporated into the political family of Georgia, cannot calculate on becoming at once the Randolphs of the State."[87] Southern Indians, therefore, became early victims of the legal institutionalization of racism that became the hallmark of the South for well over a century after the expulsion of most Indians from the region.

Ultimately, the five large southern Indian nations, the Cherokees, Chickasaws, Choctaws, Creeks, and Seminoles, signed treaties of varying legitimacy, all of which the United States Senate ratified, and moved west of the Mississippi. They rebuilt their homes, schools, and churches and reestablished their governments. But they could not escape the racism that had driven them from their homelands in the Southeast. Indeed racism intensified throughout the nineteenth century, and while African Americans were the pri-

mary victims of the violence that it engendered, Indian societies suffered almost irreparable harm. In the 1890s, the United States government allotted the holdings of southern Indians and destroyed
their nations in Oklahoma, the land that had been promised them
in perpetuity.[88] In the process of doing so, agents compiled elab-
orate rolls listing individuals and their "blood quantum," and legislation imposed restrictions on allotments on the basis of an individual's "blood quantum." The higher the "quantum" of Indian
"blood," the more stringent the restrictions since the assumption
was that "full-bloods" were less likely to understand how to manage their property than "mixed bloods." Ancestry was still an unre-
liable measure of acculturation, however, and many of those freed
from restrictions lost their land. By 1949, the southern Indians in
Oklahoma held on to less than 7 percent of their original domain.[89]
Despite the circumstances under which these racial determinations
were made—the dispossession of southern Indians—allotment rolls
with their "blood quantum" became the basis of modern tribal
membership, and in a great historical irony, the language of blood
permeates tribal politics into the twenty-first century.

Southern historians should not be surprised that the concern with
"blood" that Indians throughout the nation now share originated in
the antebellum South where the economic, social, and political system rested on the enslavement of one race by another. The legacy
of slavery was a regional obsession with race as the signifier of
power. The father of southern history, Ulrich B. Phillips, identified
"the cardinal test of a Southerner and the central theme of Southern history" as "a common resolve indomitably maintained—that
it shall be and remain a white man's country."[90] While Phillips's
scholarly reputation rests primarily on *American Negro Slavery* and
Life and Labor in the Old South, his first work, published in 1902, focused largely on Indian removal, and he established the paradigm
on which subsequent scholarship primarily has rested.[91] Reflect-

ing the views of Andrew Jackson and his contemporaries, Phillips wrote that "the average member of the tribe was heavy and stupid; but the nation was under the complete control of its chiefs, who were usually half-breeds, or white men married into the nation."[92] Race and power were inseparable.

As the decades passed, some scholars began to read the sources more critically, but "blood" continued to figure prominently in their narratives of the removal era. They reached conclusions about Native people that reflected the racial determinism of Jackson and Phillips. Angie Debo indirectly referred to "the mixed blood ascendancy that had been so apparent in Choctaw councils just before the removal,"[93] and in her work on the Creeks, she associated culture change with mixed ancestry: "A few individuals, mostly mixed bloods, began to establish farms after the white man's custom." She characterized the followers of William McIntosh, who immigrated west of the Mississippi in 1827, as "prosperous mixed-bloods, who began with their slaves to lay out plantations."[94] Henry Thompson Malone attributed Cherokee "civilization" to "the presence of a large number of influential whites and mixed-breeds" and their republic to "young mixed-blood progressives [who] acquired power in the Cherokee government."[95]

No one, however, embraced racial determinism quite as completely as Arrell M. Gibson, who taught at the University of Oklahoma for many years and trained a number of prominent modern scholars of Native America. In *The Chickasaws,* a chapter entitled "Twilight of the Full Bloods" demonstrates that in the period from 1786 to 1818 the "mixed bloods were on the threshold, ready to move in and take over management of tribal affairs." Soon they "learned to control the full bloods and to manage them to their purpose." The Great Warrior Tishomingo, according to Gibson, was "the unwitting tool of the mixed blood clique." Native people simply did not have the intellect, sophistication, or constancy to withstand a challenge by the "mixed bloods," and the "mixed bloods" duped the "full-bloods" into supporting policies that largely benefited the economic elite, that is, themselves. In order to accomplish this subtle coup, they "operate[d] through the mechanism of tribal institutions, . . . defended and preserved the form if not the substance of the old ways, . . . [and] passionately attached themselves to the practice of common ownership of tribal land."[96] While Gibson thoroughly documented "mixed blood" adherence to traditional practices, he offered no evidence for his contention that their intent was to subjugate the "full-bloods." Nor does he consider the possibility, convincingly supported by the evidence, that they actually believed in "tribal institutions, . . . the old ways, . . . [and] common ownership of tribal land." The triumph of the "mixed bloods" was as inevitable in Gibson's writings as it was in nineteenth-century rhetoric. "Mixed bloods" had a claim on power that could not be separated from their race.

William G. McLoughlin, a very fine scholar of the Cherokees who had impeccable liberal credentials, consistently used the language of blood in his work although he recognized the problems with doing so. He clarified his meaning so that his readers would not assume that he accepted genetic determinism: "Commonly understood, the difference between a full-blood and a mixed-blood was not biological or ancestral; a full-blood meant someone whose cradle language was Cherokee (and for whom Cherokee remained the primary, if not only, language). A mixed-blood was a Cherokee whose cradle language was English and for whom it remained the first and only language." McLoughlin then enumerated a variety of ways in which "mixed bloods" and "full-bloods" differed: "The mixed-bloods favored rapid acculturation, behaved like whites, and brought their children up by white values. Full-bloods kept as many of their old ways and values as they could."[97] Although McLoughlin tried to separate these terms from their literal meanings, he could not pry them out of their historical context, and they eerily echo the words of missionaries, federal agents, and politicians in the 1820s, words that undermined the governments of southern Indians and discredited their right to self-determination.

In *The New Order of Things: Property, Power, and the Transformation of the Creek Indians, 1733–1816,* an admirable book in many ways, Claudio Saunt insisted that he, too, did "not mean to imply that culture and biology are linked." Sensitive to the politics of language, he used the Spanish term *mestizo* instead of "mixed blood," but his analysis rested on what he saw as "a strong correlation . . . between the response of Creeks to the new order and their family background."[98] The "new order" produced a class system in which economic values as well as material wealth distinguished individuals, but in his sophisticated analysis of class, Saunt described the elite as *mestizo,* implying an intrinsic connection between ancestry and class that leaves little room for wealthy "full-bloods" or poor *mestizos.* Furthermore, he implied that when the *mestizo* elite engaged in the market economy, bought slaves, and became wealthy, they ceased to be culturally Indian. More thoroughly researched, carefully crafted, and convincingly argued than *The Chickasaws, The New Order of Things* nevertheless arrived at some of the same conclusions: the *mestizos,* a self-conscious group within Creek society, took control. Although Saunt disavowed the language of race in the same way as McLoughlin, he much more thoroughly convoluted race and culture to the point that race seems to determine cultural orientation in his work.[99]

Saunt saw parallels between his work and that of Melissa Meyer.[100] Meyer has written about the disruptive role of "mixed blood" people on the White Earth Anishinaabe reservation in Minnesota, but this society is not analogous to the Creeks or other southern Indians because the Anishinaabe, or Ojibwe, are patrilineal rather than matrilineal. Patrilineality meant that the children of white fathers and Indian mothers had no place in Ojibwe society because they had no clan kin, whereas in the Southeast, matrilineality made such children fully accepted members of their societies. Patrilineal peoples excluded "mixed blood" or *métis* individuals whose fathers were white, while matrilineal peoples made no distinction between them and anyone else whose mother belonged to one of the tribe's clans. Saunt's concern with class and race apparently blinded him to this important cultural distinction.

A patrilineal explanation for "mixed blood" behavior in the Southeast conforms to patriarchal European expectations as well. Such an explanation, however, not only leads us down the wrong road, but it also privileges European cultural norms and male power over the indigenous cultures of southeastern Indians in which women had considerable authority over children and households. In attributing the economic and political power of "mixed bloods" solely to the influence of white fathers, the father's European culture overwhelms the mother's Native culture. When this contest of cultures is articulated in the language of blood—"mixed bloods" versus "full-bloods"—it leaves the indelible impression that whiteness is inherently more powerful and that the history of southern Indians (and of southerners generally) was racially determined. Whites are wealthier and more politically powerful, not because they took Indian land and enslaved African people, but because they are superior. Perpetuating the language of blood denigrates the centrality of Native culture and the significance of individual choice. Reducing people to the simplistic category of race denies their imagination, their volition, and their uniqueness. In short, it denies their humanity.

In the removal crisis, Indian leaders had resisted Andrew Jackson's use of race to describe and enforce power relationships. When these leaders proclaimed an Indian identity in a region where political and economic power rested on the subjugation of non-whites, they posed an ideological threat to whites; they had demonstrated that they could govern themselves, achieve economic prosperity, create a vibrant intellectual life, and defend their rights. Attempts to reconcile ideology with reality demanded the rhetorical creation of "designing half-breeds" who manipulated and oppressed the "full-bloods." When "mixed blood" leaders rejected this construction of race, they rebuked not only the Jacksonians but also subsequent generations that have embraced a racial interpretation of their history. Although scattered Native communities persisted, by 1840 the large Indian nations with tribal landholdings were gone from the Southeast. What remained was the use of race as a classificatory tool to establish relationships of dominance and subordination. This legacy perpetuates the tragedy of removal and links us still to that sordid chapter in southern history.

Notes

One. "In the Indian Manner"

1. William Bartram, "Travels Through North and South Carolina," in *William Bartram on the Southeastern Indians*, ed. Gregory A. Waselkov and Kathryn E. Holland Braund (Lincoln: University of Nebraska Press, 1995), 46–47 (hereafter referred to as Waselkov and Braund, *William Bartram*).

2. Samuel Cole Williams, ed. *Early Travels in the Tennessee Country, 1540–1800* (Johnson City, Tenn.: The Watauga Press, 1928), 150–55.

3. Jean-Bernard Bossu, *Jean-Bernard Bossu's Travels in the Interior of North America, 1751–1762*, ed. Seymour Feiler (Norman: University of Oklahoma Press, 1962), 67.

4. George Strother Gaines, *The Reminiscences of George Strother Gaines, Pioneer and Statesman of Early Alabama and Mississippi, 1805–1843*, ed. James P. Pate (Tuscaloosa: University of Alabama Press, 1998), 47.

5. W. David Baird, *Peter Pitchlynn: Chief of the Choctaws* (Norman: University of Oklahoma Press, 1972), 5.

6. James Axtell, "The White Indians of Colonial America," in *The European and the Indian: Essays in the Ethnohistory of Colonial North America* (Oxford: Oxford University Press, 1981), 168–206.

7. J. Leitch Wright Jr., *William Augustus Bowles: Director General of the Creek Nation* (Athens: University of Georgia Press, 1967); Knox Mellon Jr., "Christian Priber's Cherokee 'Kingdom of Paradise,'" *Georgia Historical Quarterly* 57 (1973): 319–31; Claudio Saunt, *A New Order of Things: Property, Power, and the Transformation of the Creek Indians, 1733–1816* (Cambridge: Cambridge University Press, 1999), 111–38.

8. Account of Nathaniel Folsom, June 1823, in Horatio B. Cushman, *History of the Choctaw, Chickasaw, and Natchez Indians,* ed. Angie Debo (1899; reprint, Norman: University of Oklahoma Press, 1999), 326.

9. Saunt, *A New Order,* 130–33. One of the strengths of Saunt's book is his treatment of African Americans among the Creeks.

10. The information on this case is in two documents, an affidavit and a court decree (18 October 1833), in the Cherokee Supreme Court Docket, Tennessee State Archives, Nashville, Tenn. For an analysis, see Theda Perdue, "Clan and Court: Another Look at the Early Cherokee Republic," *American Indian Quarterly* 24 (2000): 562–69.

11. James Merrell, "The Racial Education of the Catawba Indians," *Journal of Southern History* 50 (1984): 363–84.

12. Theda Perdue, *Slavery and the Evolution of Cherokee Society, 1540–1866* (Knoxville: University of Tennessee Press, 1979), 36–42; Saunt, *A New Order,* 111–38.

13. William S. Willis Jr., "Divide and Rule: Red, White, and Black in the Old South," in *Red, White, and Black: Symposium on Indians in the Old South,* ed. Charles Hudson (Athens: University of Georgia Press, 1971), 99–115.

14. John Norton, *The Journal of Major John Norton, 1816,* ed. Carl Frederick Klinck and James John Talman (Toronto: Champlain Society, 1970), 45.

15. Benjamin Hawkins, "A Sketch of the Creek Country in the Years 1798 and 1799," in *Letters, Journals, and Writings of Benjamin Hawkins,* ed. C. L. Grant (Savannah: Beehive Press, 1980), 1: 292 (hereafter referred to as Grant, *Writings of Hawkins*).

16. David Taitt, "Journal of David Taitt's Travels from Pensacola, West Florida, to and Through the Country of the Upper and the Lower Creeks, 1772," in *Travels in the American Colonies,* ed. Newton D. Mereness (New York: Macmillan Company, 1916), 558.

17. Florette Henri, *The Southern Indians and Benjamin Hawkins, 1796–1816* (Norman: University of Oklahoma Press, 1986), 127.

18. Deposition of James Ore, 16 June 1792, *American State Papers: Indian Affairs* (Washington: Gales and Seaton, 1832–1861), 1: 274; John P. Brown, *Old Frontiers: The Story of the Cherokee Indians from the Earliest Times to the Date of Their Removal to the West, 1838* (Kingsport, Tenn.: Southern Publishers, Inc., 1938), 340–42.

19. Williams, *Early Travels;* Perdue, *Slavery,* 8–9.

20. For an example, see A Return of Persons Killed, Wounded, and Taken Prisoner, 5 November 1792, *American State Papers,* 1: 329–31.

21. Norton, *Journal,* 38, 49, 55.

22. Adriane Strenk, "Tradition and Transformation: Shoe Boots and the Creation of a Cherokee Culture" (master's thesis, University of Kentucky, 1993).

23. For a wonderful account of a New England woman who remained with Indians in Canada, see John Demos, *The Unredeemed Captive: A Family Story from Early America* (New York: Alfred A. Knopf, 1994). Also see James Axtell, "The White Indians of Colonial America," *William and Mary Quarterly* 32 (1975): 55–88.

24. Taitt, "Journal of Travels," 558.

25. Cushman, *History of Indians,* 375.

26. Hawkins, "Sketch of Creek Country," 1: 305; Henri, *Southern Indians,* 127, 147.

27. John Phillip Reid, "A Perilous Rule: The Law of International Homicide," in *The Cherokee Indian Nation: A Troubled History,* ed. Duane H. King (Knoxville: University of Tennessee Press, 1979), 33–45.

28. Joseph Martin, "Journal Kept by General Joseph Martin describing Hopewell Treaties with the Southern Indian Nations" (Draper Manuscript Collection, State Historical Society of Wisconsin, Madison, ser. U, vol. 14), 79; Greg O'Brien, "The Conqueror Meets the Unconquered: Negotiating Cultural Boundaries on the Post-Revolutionary Southern Frontier," *Journal of Southern History* 67 (2001): 59.

29. James Taylor Carson, *Searching for the Bright Path: The Mississippi Choctaws from Prehistory to Removal* (Lincoln: University of Nebraska Press, 1999), 22–23, 57.

30. "A Ranger's Report of Travels with General Oglethorpe, 1739–1742," in *Travels in the American Colonies,* ed. Newton D. Mereness (New York: Macmillan Company, 1916), 220; Taitt, "Journal of Travels," 502–3.

31. George Chicken, "Colonel Chicken's Journal to the Cherokees, 1725," in *Travels in the American Colonies,* ed. Newton D. Mereness (New York: Macmillan Company, 1916), 101–2.

32. Bartram, "Travels Through North and South Carolina," 50.

33. Greg O'Brien, "Choctaws in a Revolutionary Age: A Study of Power and Authority, 1750–1801" (Ph.D. diss., University of Kentucky, 1998), 46–47.

34. K. G. Davies, ed., *Documents of the American Revolution, 1700–1783* (Shannon: Irish University Press, 1972–1981), 3: 213. Thanks to Kathryn E. Holland Braund for calling this to my attention.

35. Caleb Swan, "Position and State of Manners and Arts in the Creek, or Muskogee Nation in 1791," in Henry Rowe Schoolcraft, *Historical and Statistical Information Respecting the History, Condition, and Prospects of the Indian Tribes of the United States* (Philadelphia: Lippincott, Grambo, 1851–1857), 5: 279, 281. Thanks to Claudio Saunt for pointing this out.

36. Emmet Starr, *History of the Cherokee Indians and Their Legends and Folk Lore* (Muskogee, Okla.: Hoffman Printing Co., 1984), 467.

37. "Ranger's Report," 221.

38. John Lawson, *A New Voyage to Carolina,* ed. Hugh Talmage Lefler (Chapel Hill: University of North Carolina Press, 1967), 24.

39. Bernard Romans, *A Concise and Natural History of East and West Florida,* ed. Kathryn E. Holland Braund (Tuscaloosa: University of Alabama Press, 1999), 113.

40. Hawkins, Journal, 2 April 1802, in Grant, *Writings of Hawkins,* 2: 419.

41. Hawkins, "Sketch of Creek Country," 1: 292; Hawkins, Journal, 9 February 1802, in Grant, *Writings of Hawkins,* 2: 411.

42. James Adair, *Adair's History of the American Indians,* ed. Samuel Cole Williams (1775; reprint, New York: Promontory Press, 1930), 96–97.

43. Bartram, "Observations on the Creek and Cherokee Indians," in Waselkov and Braund, *William Bartram,* 147.

44. Tobias Fitch, "Captain [Tobias] Fitch's Journal to the Creeks, 1725," in *Travels in the American Colonies,* ed. Newton D. Mereness (New York: Macmillan Company, 1916), 176.

45. The classic work on the southern Indian trade is Verner Crane, *The Southern Frontier, 1670–1732* (Durham: Duke University Press, 1928). Recent works that take a more ethnohistorical approach are John Phillip Reid, *A Better Kind of Hatchet: Law, Trade, and Diplomacy in the Cherokee Nation during the Early Years of European Contact* (University Park: Penn State University Press, 1976); Richard White, *The Roots of Dependency: Subsistence,*

Environment, and Social Change among the Choctaws, Pawnees, and Navajos (Lincoln: University of Nebraska Press, 1983), 1–146; Tom Hatley, *The Dividing Paths: Cherokees and South Carolinians Through the Era of Revolution* (New York and Oxford: Oxford University Press, 1993); and Kathryn E. Holland Braund, *Deerskins & Duffels: The Creek Indian Trade with Anglo-America, 1685–1815* (Lincoln: University of Nebraska Press, 1993).

46. Taitt to John Stuart, 16 March 1772, in Taitt, "Journal of Travels," 525, (n. 1).

47. Lawson, *New Voyage,* 190.

48. Ibid.

49. Ibid., 35–36.

50. Bossu, *Jean-Bernard Bossu,* 172; Louis-Philippe, *Diary of My Travels in America,* trans. Stephen Becker (New York: Delacorte Press, 1976), 73.

51. Taitt to Stuart, 4 May 1772, in Taitt, "Journal of Travels," 552, n 1.

52. Captain Raymond Demere to Governor William Henry Lyttleton, 24 June 1756, 2 January 1757, in *Documents Relating to Indian Affairs, 1754–1765,* ed. William L. McDowell Jr. (Columbia: South Carolina Dept. of Archives & History, 1992), 126–27, 303. Hawkins, Journal, 28 November 1796, in Grant, *Writings of Hawkins,* 1: 4.

53. Hawkins to Thomas Jefferson, 11 July 1803, in Grant, *Writings of Hawkins,* 2: 455–56.

54. Bartram, "Observations on the Creek and Cherokee Indians," 155–56.

55. Hawkins, Journal, 20 December 1796, in Grant, *Writings of Hawkins,* 1: 25.

56. Bartram, "Travels Through North and South Carolina," 77.

57. Hawkins, Journal, 25 December 1796, in Grant, *Writings of Hawkins,* 1: 28.

58. Hawkins, Journal, 18, 25 December 1796, in Grant, *Writings of Hawkins,* 1: 22, 27–28.

59. Taitt, "Journal of Travels," 504–5.

60. Bartram, "Travels Through North and South Carolina," 65–66.

61. Lawson, *New Voyage,* 192.

62. See James Crawford, *The Mobilian Trade Language* (Knoxville: University of Tennessee Press, 1978).

63. Adair, *Adair's History,* 398.

64. Lawson, *New Voyage,* 192.

65. For a discussion of these traditional practices, see Charles Hudson, *The Southeastern Indians* (Knoxville: University of Tennessee Press, 1976), 317–18, 365–75.

66. Hawkins, Journal, 18 December 1796, 1: 22.

67. Adair, *Adair's History,* 251.

68. Ibid., 39.

69. Ibid., 92, 259.

70. The best study of kinship among southern Indians is John Phillip Reid, *A Law of Blood: The Primitive Law of the Cherokee Nation* (New York: New York University Press, 1970).

71. Norton, *Journal,* 36, 66.

72. Thomas Nairne, *Nairne's Muskhogean Journals: The 1708 Expedition to the Mississippi River,* ed. Alexander Moore (Jackson: University Press of Mississippi, 1988), 60–61.

73. Lawson, *New Voyage,* 192.

74. Traders themselves sometimes precipitated or contributed to hostilities. The Tuscarora War (1711–1713) and the Yamassee War (1715), which claimed the lives of most of the traders among southern Indians except those in Cherokee country, are notable examples of wars caused in part by trade issues. See Crane, *Southern Frontier,* 158–61, 162–86; Adair, *Adair's History,* 281–83.

75. Henry Timberlake, *Lieut. Henry Timberlake's Memoirs, 1756–1765,* ed. Samuel Cole Williams (Johnson City, Tenn.: Watauga Press, 1927), 89.

76. Bartram, "Travels Through North and South Carolina," 96; Brown, *Old Frontiers,* 348.

77. Bartram, "Travels Through North and South Carolina," 46–47.

78. Hawkins, Announcement, 14 January 1799, in Grant, *Writings of Hawkins,* 1: 239.

79. Hawkins to Jefferson, 11 July 1803, 2: 455–56.

80. Hawkins, Journal, 18 December 1796, 1: 21.

81. Michael D. Green, "Mary Musgrove: Creating a New World," in *Sifters: Native American Women's Lives,* ed. Theda Perdue (New York and Oxford: Oxford University Press, 2001), 29.

82. Starr, *History of Cherokee,* 468–71; Brown, *Old Frontiers,* 275.

83. Brown, *Old Frontiers,* 277–78, 348.

84. Bartram, "Travels Through North and South Carolina," 46.

85. Gaines, *Reminiscences of Gaines,* 47.

86. Cushman, *History of Indians,* 328.

87. Lawson, *New Voyage,* 35–36.

88. Hawkins, Journal, 16 February 1797, in Grant, *Writings of Hawkins,* 1: 47.

89. Hawkins, "Sketch of Creek Country," 1: 301.

90. Bartram, "Travels Through North and South Carolina," 114.

91. Romans, *Concise and Natural History,* 147; Louis-Philippe, *Diary of Travels,* 72.

92. Theda Perdue, "Native Women in the Early Republic: Old World Perceptions, New World Realities," in *Native Americans in the Early Republic,* ed. Ronald Hoffman and Frederick Hoxie (Charlottesville: University of Virginia Press, 1999), 85–122.

93. Bartram, "Travels Through North and South Carolina," 101–2.

94. Hawkins to addressee unknown, n.d., in Grant, *Writings of Hawkins,* 2: 457.

95. Adair, *Adair's History,* 133–35.

96. Bartram, "Travels Through North and South Carolina," 47.

97. Lawson, *New Voyage,* 195.

98. Adair, *Adair's History,* 447–48.

99. Hawkins, Journal, 11 December 1796, in Grant, *Writings of Hawkins,* 1: 15.

100. Norton, *Journal,* 76, 121.

101. Joe M. Anoatubby, "Debunking the Mixed-Blood Myth: Alternatives for Interpreting Chickasaw History," (paper presented at the Southern Historical Association, Louisville, Ky., 2000).

102. Quoted in Nathaniel J. Sheidley, "Unruly Men: Indians, Settlers, and the Ethos of Frontier Patriarchy in the Upper Tennessee Watershed, 1763–1815" (Ph.D. diss., Princeton University, 1999), 155–67.

103. U.S. Commissioners to Secretary Graham, 8 July 1817, *Correspondence of Andrew Jackson, 1767–1845,* ed. John S. Bassett (Washington: Carnegie Institution, 1926–35), 2: 300.

104. David Keith Hampton, comp., *Cherokee Reservees* (Oklahoma City: Baker Publishing Co., 1979).

105. Petition, 30 June 1818, in Papers of the American Board of Commissioners for Foreign Missions, Houghton Library, Harvard University, Cambridge, Mass. (hereafter referred to as ABCFM). Reprinted in Theda Perdue and Michael D. Green, *The Cherokee Removal: A Brief History with Documents* (Boston: Bedford Books, 1995), 125.

106. Theda Perdue, *Cherokee Women: Gender and Culture Change, 1700–1835* (Lincoln: University of Nebraska Press, 1998), 153–55.

107. *Laws of the Cherokee Nation: Adopted by the Council at Various Periods. Printed for the Benefit of the Nation* (Tahlequah, Cherokee Nation: Cherokee Advocate Office, 1852), 10.

108. Antonio J. Waring, ed., *Laws of the Creek Nation* (Athens: University of Georgia Press, 1960), 20, 22, 26.

109. Swan, "Position and State," 262–63.

110. Romans, *Concise and Natural History,* 137.

111. William G. McLoughlin and Walter H. Conser Jr., "The Cherokee Censuses of 1809, 1825, and 1835," in McLoughlin, *The Cherokee Ghost Dance: Essays on the Southeastern Indians, 1789–1861* (Macon: Mercer University Press, 1984), 218, 240.

112. Arrell M. Gibson, *The Chickasaws* (Norman: University of Oklahoma Press, 1971), estimated that one quarter of the Chickasaws were "mixed bloods," a proportion similar to the Cherokees, but he did not list the number of resident whites (142). The Armstrong Roll [ed. Larry S. Watson (Laguna Hills, Calif.: Histree, 1985)], made in preparation for removal, listed 151 whites and nearly eighteen thousand Choctaws, but it did not enumerate "mixed bloods."

113. Hawkins to addressee unknown, 2: 457.

Two. *"Both White and Red"*

1. John P. Brown, *Old Frontiers: The Story of the Cherokee Indians from the Earliest Times to the Date of Their Removal to the West, 1838* (Kingsport, Tenn.: Southern Publishers, Inc., 1938), 128.

2. Cameron was not alone in begetting children by Native women, and the question of identity extended far beyond his son. A similar grant in 1737 from the Yamacraw chief Tomochichi to Mary Musgrove, whose father was an English trader and mother was Creek, did not reach resolution for two decades—and then she lost the grant to Yamacraw Bluff but settled for title to St. Catherine's Island, which she received from her Creek kinsman Malatchi. Michael D. Green, "Mary Musgrove: Creating a New World," in *Sifters: Native American Women's Lives,* ed. Theda Perdue (New York and Oxford: Oxford University Press, 2001), 35, 45.

3. Duane Champagne makes this point briefly in *Social Order and Political Change: Constitutional Governments among the Cherokee, the Choctaw, the Chickasaw, and the Creek* (Stanford: Stanford University Press, 1992), 54.

4. John Lawson, *A New Voyage to Carolina,* ed. Hugh Talmage Lefler (Chapel Hill: University of North Carolina Press, 1967), 192.

5. Hawkins to James McHenry, 6 January 1797, in *Letters, Journals, and Writings of Benjamin Hawkins,* ed. C. L. Grant (Savannah: Beehive Press, 1980) 1: 63 (hereafter referred to as Grant, *Writings of Hawkins*).

6. Rufus Anderson, *Memoir of Catharine Brown: A Christian Indian of the Cherokee Nation* (Boston: Crocker and Brewster; New York: John P. Haven, 1825; reprint, Signal Mountain, Tenn.: Mountain Press, 1998), 124.

7. John Norton, *The Journal of Major John Norton, 1816,* ed. Carl Frederick Klinck and James John Talman (Toronto: Champlain Society, 1970), 60.

8. William Bartram, "Travels Through North and South Carolina," in *William Bartram on the Southeastern Indians,* ed. Gregory A. Waselkov and Kathryn E. Holland Braund (Lincoln: University of Nebraska Press, 1995), 102 (hereafter referred to as Waselkov and Braund, *William Bartram*).

9. Brainerd Journal, 5, 23 September, 20 October 1818; Daniel S. Butrick's Journal, 6 October 1818; both in Papers of the American Board of Commissioners for Foreign Missions, Houghton Library, Harvard University, Cambridge, Mass. (hereafter referred to as ABCFM).

10. Hawkins, Journal, 16 February 1797, in Grant, *Writings of Hawkins,* 1: 47–48.

11. In "A Sketch of the Creek Country in the Years 1798 and 1799," Hawkins identifies the uncle as Sam Macnac. Perhaps he meant Sam Moniac. Benjamin Hawkins, "A Sketch of the Creek Country in the Years 1798

and 1799," in Grant, *Writings of Hawkins,* 1: 298. But in 1809, he wrote that the daughters' guardian was Sam Menawa. Hawkins to William Eustis, 27 August 1809, in Grant, *Writings of Hawkins,* 2: 556.

12. Louis-Philippe, *Diary of My Travels in America,* trans. Stephen Becker (New York: Delacorte Press, 1976), 76–77.

13. "Journal of David Taitt's Travels from Pensacola, West Florida, to and Through the Country of the Upper and Lower Creeks, 1772"; "Colonel [George] Chicken's Journal to the Cherokees, 1725"; "A Ranger's Report of Travels with General Oglethorpe, 1739–1742"; in *Travels in the American Colonies,* ed. Newton D. Mereness (New York: Macmillan Company, 1916), 541, 224, 135.

14. Taitt, "Journal of Travels," 510.

15. Hawkins, Journal, 21 January 1797, in Grant, *Writings of Hawkins,* 1: 37.

16. In his dissertation, "The Invention of the Creek Nation: A Political History of the Creek Indians in the South's Imperial Era, 1540–1763" (Ph.D. diss., Emory University, 2000), Steven C. Hahn maintained that chiefly descent among the Creeks was patrilineal. His views reflect those of William S. Willis Jr., "Patrilineal Institutions in Southeastern North America," *Ethnohistory* 10 (1963): 250–69. While a few documents support this interpretation, the preponderance of the evidence, in my opinion, as well as that of other southeastern ethnohistorians, does not.

17. Thomas Nairne, *Nairne's Muskhogean Journals: The 1708 Expedition to the Mississippi River,* ed. Alexander Moore (Jackson: University Press of Mississippi, 1988), 61–62.

18. Lawson, *New Voyage,* 205.

19. Hawkins, "A Sketch of Creek Country," 1: 318.

20. Taitt, "Journal of Travels," 504–5.

21. Brown, *Old Frontiers,* 277–78, 332, 345–46, 353.

22. Louis-Philippe, *Diary of Travels,* 77.

23. For policy in this period, see Reginald Horsman, *Expansion and American Indian Policy, 1783–1812* (East Lansing: Michigan State University Press, 1967).

24. Hawkins to Peter Early, 15 February 1815, in Grant, *Writings of Hawkins,* 2: 717.

25. J. Leitch Wright Jr., *Creeks and Seminoles: The Destruction and Regener-*

ation of the Muscogulge People (Lincoln: University of Nebraska Press, 1986), 60, 167–68.

26. Hawkins to James Monroe, 23 January 1815, in Grant, *Writings of Hawkins,* 2: 716–17.

27. See Michael D. Green, *The Politics of Indian Removal: Creek Government and Society in Crisis* (Lincoln: University of Nebraska Press, 1982); Joel W. Martin, *Sacred Revolt: The Muskogees' Struggle for a New World* (Boston: Beacon Press, 1991); Gregory Evans Dowd, *A Spirited Resistance: The North American Indian Struggle for Unity, 1745–1815* (Baltimore: Johns Hopkins University Press, 1992); Claudio Saunt, *A New Order of Things: Property, Power, and the Transformation of the Creek Indians, 1733–1816* (Cambridge: Cambridge University Press, 1999).

28. James Taylor Carson, *Searching for the Bright Path: The Mississippi Choctaws from Prehistory to Removal* (Lincoln: University of Nebraska Press, 1999), 86–102.

29. Green, *Politics,* 69–97; "Treaty with the Creeks, 1825," in Charles J. Kappler, ed., *Indian Treaties, 1778–1883* (1904; reprint, New York: Amereon House, 1972), 214–17.

30. Carson, *Searching for Path,* 70.

31. W. David Baird, *Peter Pitchlynn: Chief of the Choctaws* (Norman: University of Oklahoma Press, 1972), 24–28.

32. Gary E. Moulton, *John Ross: Cherokee Chief* (Athens: University of Georgia Press, 1978), 6.

33. Benjamin W. Griffith Jr., *McIntosh and Weatherford: Creek Indian Leaders* (Tuscaloosa: University of Alabama Press, 1988), 254.

34. Carson, *Searching for Path,* 95–96; Donna L. Akers, "Peter P. Pitchlynn: Race and Identity in Nineteenth-Century America," in *The Human Tradition in Antebellum America,* ed. Michael A. Morrison (Wilmington, Del.: Scholarly Resources, 2000), 134. Baird *(Peter Pitchlynn,* 6) wrote that John Pitchlynn married daughters of Ebenezer and Nathaniel Folsom. For a discussion of the conflicting evidence, see James Taylor Carson's dissertation, "Searching for the Bright Path: The Mississippi Choctaws from Prehistory to Removal" (Ph.D. diss., University of Kentucky, 1996), 128–29, rather than his book. All other references in this book are to Carson's book.

35. Arturo O'Neill to Josef de Ezpeleta, 19 October 1783, in John Walton

Caughey, *McGillivray of the Creeks* (Norman: University of Oklahoma Press, 1938), 62–63.

36. Horatio B. Cushman, *History of the Choctaw, Chickasaw, and Natchez Indians,* ed. Angie Debo (1899; reprint, Norman: University of Oklahoma Press, 1999) 355; Champagne, *Social Order,* 156–84; William G. McLoughlin, *After the Trail of Tears: The Cherokees' Struggle for Sovereignty, 1839–1880* (Chapel Hill: University of North Carolina Press, 1993), 229. John Ross's sister Elizabeth married John Golden Ross, who was not related. Emmet Starr, *History of the Cherokee Indians and Their Legends and Folk Lore* (Muskogee, Okla.: Hoffman Printing Co., 1984), 410–11.

37. Joe M. Anoatubby, "Debunking the Mixed-Blood Myth: Alternatives for Interpreting Chickasaw History," (paper presented at the Southern Historical Association, Louisville, Ky., 2000).

38. William G. McLoughlin, *Cherokee Renascence in the New Republic* (Princeton: Princeton University Press, 1986), 191–92.

39. Carson, *Searching for Path,* 92–93, 102.

40. William G. McLoughlin, "Thomas Jefferson and the Rise of Cherokee Nationalism, 1806–1809," in *The Cherokee Ghost Dance: Essays on the Southeastern Indians* (Macon, Ga.: Mercer University Press, 1984), 73–110 (hereafter referred to as McLoughlin, *Cherokee Ghost Dance*).

41. Thurman Wilkins, *Cherokee Tragedy: The Ridge Family and the Decimation of a People* (New York: Macmillan, 1970), 253.

42. Chester B. DePratter, *Late Prehistoric and Early Historic Chiefdoms in the Southeastern United States* (New York: Garland Publishing, 1991); Timothy R. Pauketat, *The Ascent of Chiefs: Cahokia and Mississippian Politics in Native North America* (Tuscaloosa: University of Alabama Press, 1994); John E. Scarry, ed., *Political Structure and Change in the Prehistoric Southeastern United States* (Gainesville: University Presses of Florida, 1996); Bruce D. Smith, ed., *Mississippian Emergence: The Evolution of Ranked Agricultural Societies in Eastern North America* (Washington, D.C.: Smithsonian Institution Press, 1990); Mark Williams and Gary Shapiro, eds., *Lamar Archaeology: Mississippian Chiefdoms in the Deep South* (Tuscaloosa: University of Alabama Press, 1990).

43. Lawson, *New Voyage,* 200.

44. Carson, *Searching for Path,* 14–15.

45. Bartram, "Observations on the Creek and Cherokee Indians," in Waselkov and Braund, *William Bartram,* 147.

46. Bartram, "Travels Through North and South Carolina," 53.

47. Grant Foreman, *Advancing the Frontier, 1830–1860* (Norman: University of Oklahoma Press, 1933), 324–25.

48. Richard White, *The Roots of Dependency: Subsistence, Environment, and Social Change among the Choctaws, Pawnees, and Navajos* (Lincoln: University of Nebraska Press, 1983), 34–51.

49. Theda Perdue, *Cherokee Women: Gender and Culture Change, 1700–1835* (Lincoln: University of Nebraska Press, 1998), 102.

50. Hawkins, "Sketch of Creek Country," 1: 292.

51. Francis Paul Prucha, *American Indian Policy in the Formative Years: The Indian Trade and Intercourse Acts, 1790–1834* (Cambridge, Mass.: Harvard University Press, 1962), 41–50.

52. For examples of annuity payments, see Hawkins to Henry Dearborn, 1 January 1809, and Hawkins to William Eustis, 1812, in Grant, *Writings of Hawkins,* 2: 547, 600.

53. Hawkins, Journal, 9 February 1802, in Grant, *Writings of Hawkins,* 2: 411.

54. Henry Knox to George Washington, 7 July 1789, *American State Papers: Indian Affairs* (Washington: Gales and Seaton, 1832–1861), 1: 53.

55. Doublehead to Meigs, 8 June 1804, Pathkiller and Toolachee to Meigs, 14 September 1812, Records of the Cherokee Agency in Tennessee, 1801–1835, Record Group 75, National Archives, Washington, D.C., Microcopy M-208 (hereafter referred to as M-208).

56. Hawkins to Thomas Jefferson, 13 September 1806, in Grant, *Writings of Hawkins,* 2: 508.

57. Hawkins, Journal, 9 February 1802, 2: 410.

58. The way in which political power continued to have a spiritual base into the early nineteenth century is the subject of O'Brien's "Choctaws in a Revolutionary Age: A Study of Power and Authority, 1750–1801" (Ph.D. diss., University of Kentucky, 1998).

59. Bartram, "Travels Through North and South Carolina," 66.

60. James Axtell, *The Invasion Within: The Contest of Cultures in Colonial North America* (Oxford: Oxford University Press, 1985), 4; William G.

McLoughlin, "Native American Reactions to Christian Missions," in *The Cherokees and Christianity, 1794–1870* (Athens: University of Georgia Press, 1994), 9–33.

61. Quoted in O'Brien, "Choctaws in a Revolutionary Age," 27–28.

62. Rowena McClinton Ruff, "Notable Persons in Cherokee History: Charles Hicks," *Journal of Cherokee Studies* 17 (1996): 16–27; Lee Irwin, "Different Voices Together: Preservation and Acculturation in Early 19th Century Cherokee Religion," *Journal of Cherokee Studies* 18 (1997): 3–26.

63. Carson, *Searching for Path,* 108.

64. Clara Sue Kidwell, *Choctaws and Missionaries in Mississippi, 1818–1918* (Norman: University of Oklahoma Press, 1995), 92–115; Champagne, *Social Order,* 152.

65. Carson, *Searching for Path,* 110.

66. Arrell M. Gibson, *The Chickasaws* (Norman: University of Oklahoma Press, 1971), 103–37; Carson, *Searching for Path,* 103–26.

67. William G. McLoughlin, *Cherokees and Missionaries, 1789–1839* (New Haven: Yale University Press, 1974), 47–53, 317.

68. Ibid., 110.

69. Gibson, *Chickasaws,* 65, 110.

70. Kidwell, *Choctaws and Missionaries,* 50–68. Quote on 68.

71. Carson, *Searching for Path,* 83, 90–91.

72. *Missionary Herald,* September 1820, 417.

73. Carson, *Searching for Path,* 95.

74. Ibid., 94.

75. Quoted in McLoughlin, *Cherokees and Missionaries,* 135.

76. Anderson, *Memoir of Catharine Brown,* 10, 23.

77. John Ridge to Albert Gallatin, 27 February 1826, in Perdue and Green, *The Cherokee Removal: A Brief History with Documents* (Boston: Bedford Books, 1995), 40.

78. Nathaniel J. Sheidley, "Unruly Men: Indians, Settlers, and the Ethos of Frontier Patriarchy in the Upper Tennessee Watershed, 1763–1815" (Ph.D. diss., Princeton University, 1999), 231–51.

79. Bartram, "Observations on the Creek and Cherokee Indians," 156–58.

80. James Adair, *Adair's History of the American Indians,* ed. Samuel Cole Williams (1775; reprint, New York: Promontory Press, 1930), 443.

81. Louis-Philippe, *Diary of Travels,* 96–97.

82. Cushman says that they introduced cattle, but evidence points to the presence of cattle in the Choctaw Nation as early as 1700. Cushman, *History of Indians,* 344–45; Carson, *Searching for Path,* 54.

83. Saunt, *A New Order,* 89, 169–71.

84. Perdue, *Cherokee Women,* 140–41.

85. Norton, *Journal,* 51–52.

86. Hawkins to addressee unknown, n.d., in Grant, *Writings of Hawkins,* 2: 457; William G. McLoughlin, "Cherokee Anomie, 1794–1810," in *The Cherokee Ghost Dance: Essays on the Southeastern Indians, 1789–1861* (Macon: Mercer University Press, 1984), 3–38.

87. Thomas L. McKenney and James Hall, *The Indian Tribes of North America, with Biographical Sketches and Anecdotes of the Principal Chiefs* (Edinburgh: John Grant, 1935), 2: 178–93; "Alabama Indian Chiefs," *The Alabama Historical Quarterly* 13 (1951): 45–49.

88. James C. Kelley, "Oconostota," *Journal of Cherokee Studies* 3 (1979): 233.

89. Saunt, *A New Order,* 176–77.

90. Young Wolf's Last Will and Testament, 12 March 1814, John Howard Payne Papers, Newberry Library, Chicago, Ill.; reprinted in Perdue and Green, *Cherokee Removal,* 29.

91. McLoughlin, *Renascence,* 77–91. Quote on p. 88.

92. Saunt, *A New Order,* 217.

93. Carson, *Searching for Path,* 72.

94. Gibson, *Chickasaws,* 148–53; George Strother Gaines, *The Reminiscences of George Strother Gaines, Pioneer and Statesman of Early Alabama and Mississippi, 1805–1843,* ed. James P. Pate (Tuscaloosa: University of Alabama Press, 1998), 148.

95. Perdue, *Cherokee Women,* pt. 1.

96. Hawkins to addressee unknown, 2: 457.

97. Daniel F. Littlefield Jr., *The Chickasaw Freedmen: A People Without a Country,* (Westport, Conn.: Greenwood Press, 1980), 9–10.

98. Kidwell, *Choctaws and Missionaries,* 108–9. There were 17,963 Choctaws. Carson, *Searching for Path,* 80.

99. The 1835 census lists 16,542 Cherokees and 201 intermarried whites. William G. McLoughlin and Walter H. Conser Jr., "The Cherokee Cen-

suses of 1809, 1825, and 1835" in McLoughlin, *Cherokee Ghost Dance,* 215–50; R. Halliburton Jr., *Red Over Black: Black Slavery among the Cherokee Indians* (Westport, Conn.: Greenwood Press, 1977), 181–90. McLoughlin and Conser point out that agent Return J. Meigs overestimated the number of "mixed blood" Cherokees.

100. Littlefield, *Chickasaw Freedmen,* 10.

101. Creeks totaled 22,694. Daniel F. Littlefield, *Africans and Creeks: From the Colonial Period to the Civil War* (Westport, Conn.: Greenwood Press, 1979), 115–16.

102. *Laws of the Cherokee Nation: Adopted by the Council at Various Periods. Printed for the Benefit of the Nation* (Tahlequah, Cherokee Nation: Cherokee Advocate Office, 1852), 3.

103. Duane Champagne provides a good summary of this process in chapter 5 of *Social Order,* 124–75.

104. Green, *Politics,* 149–52.

105. Green, *Politics,* 69–97.

106. James Mooney, "Myths of the Cherokee," *19th Annual Report of the Bureau of American Ethnology* (Washington: Government Printing Office, 1900), 239.

107. Gibson, *Chickasaws,* 10–11.

108. Carson, *Searching for Path,* 8.

109. Green, *Politics,* 13.

110. *Laws of Cherokee Nation,* 118–19.

111. For a concise treatment, see Theda Perdue, "The Trail of Tears: Removal of the Southern Indians," in *The American Indian Experience: A Profile, 1524 to the Present,* ed. Phillip Weeks (Arlington Heights, Ill.: Forum Press, 1988), 96–117.

112. Florence Rebecca Ray, *Chieftain Greenwood LeFlore and the Choctaw Indians of the Mississippi Valley* (Memphis: Davis Printing Co., 1936).

113. Griffith, *McIntosh and Weatherford,* 254.

114. Sharon Flanagan, "The Georgia Cherokees Who Remained: Race, Status and Property in the Cherokee Community," *The Georgia Historical Quarterly* 73 (1989): 584–609.

115. Moulton, *John Ross,* 100–101.

Three. *"Designing Half-Breeds"*

1. Jackson to Crawford, 10 June 1816, in *Correspondence of Andrew Jackson,* ed. John S. Bassett (Washington, D.C.: Carnegie Institution, 1926–1935), 2: 244.

2. Francis Jennings, *The Invasion of America: Indians, Colonization, and the Cant of Conquest* (Chapel Hill: University of North Carolina Press, 1975), 43–57; Roy Harvey Pearce, *Savagism and Civilization: A Study of the Indian and the American Mind* (Berkeley: University of California Press, 1988), 3–49; James Axtell, *The Invasion Within: The Contest of Cultures in Colonial North America* (Oxford: Oxford University Press, 1985), 131–78.

3. Bernard W. Sheehan, *Seeds of Extinction: Jeffersonian Philanthropy and the American Indian* (Chapel Hill: University of North Carolina Press, 1973), 15–116.

4. William Byrd, *William Byrd's Histories of the Dividing Line Betwixt Virginia and North Carolina,* ed. William K. Boyd (1929; reprint, New York: Dover Publications, 1967), 120.

5. Thomas Jefferson, *Notes on the State of Virginia,* ed. William Peden (Chapel Hill: University of North Carolina Press, 1955), 62; Jefferson to Chastellux, 7 June 1785, in *The Papers of Thomas Jefferson,* ed. Julian P. Boyd et al. (Princeton: Princeton University Press, 1950) 7: 185.

6. For example, see James Adair, *Adair's History of the American Indians,* ed. Samuel Cole Williams (1775; reprint, New York: Promontory Press, 1930), 4–5.

7. Robert Beverley, *The History and Present State of Virginia* (1705, reprint, Indianapolis and New York: The Bobbs-Merrill Company, Inc. 1971), 89.

8. Sheehan, *Seeds of Extinction,* 174–80.

9. Helen C. Rountree, "Pocahontas: The Hostage Who Became Famous," in *Sifters: Native American Women's Lives,* ed. Theda Perdue (New York and Oxford: Oxford University Press, 2001) 14–28.

10. Beverley, *History of Virginia,* 18–19.

11. Byrd, *Histories of Dividing Line,* 120.

12. Wilbur R. Jacobs, *The Appalachian Indian Frontier: The Edmund Atkin Report and Plan of 1755* (1954; reprint, Lincoln: University of Nebraska Press, 1967), 80, 91 (n. 3).

13. Arturo O'Neill to Marqués de Sonora, 12 July 1787, in *McGillivray of the Creeks,* ed. John Walton Caughey (Norman: University of Oklahoma Press, 1938), 156–58.

14. Jefferson to Hawkins, 18 February 1803, in *The Writings of Thomas Jefferson,* ed. Andrew A. Lipscomb and Albert Ellery Bergh (Washington, D.C.: Thomas Jefferson Memorial Assn., 1903–1904), 10: 363.

15. Ibid.

16. *Missionary Herald,* January 1827, 9.

17. *Missionary Herald,* October 1819, 465.

18. *Missionary Herald,* September 1822, 287.

19. Byrd, *Histories of Dividing Line,* 4.

20. Hawkins to Jefferson, 11 July 1803, in *Letters, Journals, and Writings of Benjamin Hawkins,* ed. C. L. Grant (Savannah: Beehive Press, 1980), 2: 455–56 (hereafter referred to as Grant, *Writings of Hawkins*).

21. Meigs to Chulisa and Sour Mush, 14 March 1808. Records of the Cherokee Agency in Tennessee, 1801–1835, Record Group 75, National Archives, Washington, D.C., Microcopy M-208 (hereafter referred to as M-208).

22. Bernard Romans, *A Concise and Natural History of East and West Florida,* ed. Kathryn E. Holland Braund (Tuscaloosa: University of Alabama Press, 1999), 110–11.

23. Thomas L. McKenney and James Hall, *The Indian Tribes of North America, with Biographical Sketches and Anecdotes of the Principal Chiefs* (Edinburgh: John Grant, 1935), 2: 264–69.

24. Doublehead to J. D. Chisolm, 20 November 1802, M-208.

25. For the centralization of government, see Duane Champagne, *Social Order and Political Change: Constitutional Governments among the Cherokee, the Choctaw, the Chickasaw, and the Creek* (Stanford: Stanford University Press, 1992), chaps. 3 and 4. For the persistence of traditional practices, see Theda Perdue, *Cherokee Women: Gender and Culture Change, 1700–1835* (Lincoln: University of Nebraska Press, 1998), chap. 6. Rennard Strickland has examined the fusion of traditional and English common law in *Fire and the Spirits: Cherokee Law from Clan to Court* (Norman: University of Oklahoma Press, 1975).

26. William G. McLoughlin, "Native American Reactions to Christian

Missions," in *The Cherokees and Christianity, 1794–1870* (Athens: University of Georgia Press, 1994), 25.

27. James Taylor Carson, *Searching for the Bright Path: The Mississippi Choctaws from Prehistory to Removal* (Lincoln: University of Nebraska Press, 1999), 125; Arrell M. Gibson, *The Chickasaws* (Norman: University of Oklahoma Press, 1971), 135.

28. Jefferson to Hawkins, 18 February 1803, in *The Writings of Thomas Jefferson,* ed. Paul Leicester Ford (New York: G. P. Putnam's Sons, 1892–1899), 8: 213–14.

29. Draft of Jefferson's Fifth Annual Message, in *The Writings of Thomas Jefferson,* ed. Paul Leicester Ford (New York: G. P. Putnam's Sons, 1892–1899), 8: 394.

30. Meigs to Hawkins, 13 February 1805, M-208.

31. For how these changing attitudes affected Indians specifically, see Robert F. Berkhofer Jr., *The White Man's Indian: Images of the American Indian from Columbus to the Present* (New York: Random House, 1978), 33–70; Robert E. Bieder, *Science Encounters the Indian, 1820–1880* (Norman: University of Oklahoma Press, 1986); and Reginald Horsman, *Race and Manifest Destiny: The Origins of American Racial Anglo-Saxonism* (Cambridge, Mass.: Harvard University Press, 1981). For the rise of scientific racism, see Thomas F. Gossett, *Race: The History of an Idea in America* (1963; reprint, Oxford: Oxford University Press, 1997), 32–84; George M. Fredrickson, *The Black Image in the White Mind: The Debate on African American Character and Destiny, 1817–1914* (New York: Harper & Row, 1971), 1–96; and William Stanton, *The Leopard's Spots: Scientific Attitudes Toward Race in America, 1815–59* (Chicago: University of Chicago Press, 1960).

32. Romans, *Concise and Natural History,* 110.

33. Petition, 30 June 1818, in Papers of the American Board of Commissioners for Foreign Missions, Houghton Library, Harvard University, Cambridge, Mass. (hereafter referred to as ABCFM). Reprinted in Theda Perdue and Michael D. Green, *The Cherokee Removal: A Brief History with Documents* (Boston: Bedford Books, 1995), 125.

34. *Missionary Herald,* April 1830, 115.

35. Speech of the Hon. Wilson Lumpkin to the U.S. House of Representatives, May 1830, in Wilson Lumpkin, *The Removal of the Cherokee Indi-*

ans from Georgia, 1827–1841 (1907; reprint, New York: Augustus M. Kelley, 1971), 79, 82.

36. Ibid., 83.

37. Ibid., 79.

38. Lewis Cass, "Removal of the Indians," *North American Review* 30 (January 1830): 67.

39. Dana D. Nelson, *The Word in Black and White: Reading Race in American Literature, 1638–1867* (Oxford: Oxford University Press, 1993), 38–64. Quote on p. 51. Also see Berkhofer, *White Man's Indian,* 71–96; and Susan Scheckel, *The Insistence of the Indian: Race and Nationalism in Nineteenth-Century American Culture* (Princeton: Princeton University Press, 1998).

40. Quoted in Horsman, *Race and Manifest Destiny,* 58–59.

41. Ibid., 118.

42. Thomas L. McKenney, *Memoirs, Official and Personal* (1846; reprint, Lincoln: University of Nebraska Press, 1973), 188–90; J. Leitch Wright Jr., *Creeks and Seminoles: The Destruction and Regeneration of the Muscogulge People* (Lincoln: University of Nebraska Press, 1986), 231.

43. *American Eagle,* 22 March 1824; *Niles Weekly Register,* 9 July 1825. Both quoted in Thurman Wilkins, *Cherokee Tragedy: The Ridge Family and the Decimation of a People* (New York: MacMillan, 1970), 148–150.

44. Joel Williamson, *New People: Miscegenation and Mulattoes in the United States* (New York: Free Press, 1980), 71–75.

45. Quoted in Bernard W. Sheehan, *Seeds of Extinction,* 177.

46. Horsman, *Race and Manifest Destiny,* 118.

47. Speech of the Hon. Wilson Lumpkin, 70, 77.

48. Cass, "Removal of Indians," 71.

49. *Missionary Herald,* May 1822, 139.

50. Members of the Church at Brainerd exclusive of the missionaries; Members of the Church at Creek Path, May 1822; Report on the Station at Haweis, January 1828, ABCFM.

51. *Missionary Herald,* September 1824, 284.

52. *Missionary Herald,* February 1823, 45. By "native," missionaries mean "inherent" not "Indian."

53. Butrick to Jeremiah Evarts, 24 November 1824, ABCFM.

54. *Missionary Herald,* February 1829, 58.

55. *Missionary Herald,* March 1831, 82.

56. Minutes of a Conference between Brigadier General James Wilkinson, Benjamin Hawkins and Andrew Pickens, Esquires, Commissioners of the United States, and the Principal Chiefs of the Choctaw Nation of Indians, held at Fort Adams, 15 December 1801, in Grant, *Writings of Hawkins,* 1: 397–98.

57. Carson, *Searching for Path,* 79; Champagne, *Social Order,* 149.

58. Levi Colbert et. al. to Andrew Jackson, 22 November 1832, Letters Received, 1824–1881, U.S. Bureau of Indian Affairs, Record Groups 75, National Archives, Washington, D.C., Microcopy M-234 (hereafter referred to as M 234).

59. The best source for portraits of Indian men is McKenney and Hall, *Indian Tribes of North America.* For an example, see William McIntosh's portrait, 1: 261.

60. Quoted in Champagne, *Social Order,* 112.

61. McKenney and Hall, *Indian Tribes of North America,* 1: 62, 368.

62. *Missionary Herald,* September 1824, 285.

63. *Missionary Herald,* September 1824, 284.

64. *Missionary Herald,* August 1820, 380.

65. *Missionary Herald,* September 1824, 284.

66. Emmet Starr, *History of the Cherokee Indians and Their Legends and Folk Lore* (Muskogee, Okla.: Hoffman Printing Co., 1984), 426–27, 474–75.

67. Mary Jane Warde, *George Washington Grayson and the Creek Nation, 1843–1920* (Norman: University of Oklahoma Press, 1999), 14; Don L. Shadburn, *Unhallowed Intrusion: A History of Cherokee Families in Forsyth County, Georgia* (Saline, Mich.: McNaughton and Gunn, Inc., 1993), 113–14.

68. *Missionary Herald,* July 1818, 339.

69. Elias Boudinot, "An Address to the Whites," in Theda Perdue, *Cherokee Editor: The Writings of Elias Boudinot* (Knoxville: University of Tennessee Press, 1983), 69.

70. *Missionary Herald,* October 1821, 310–11.

71. Warde, *Grayson,* 4.

72. McKenney, *Memoirs,* 38.

73. William Chamberlain's Journal, 24 August 1825; Samuel A. Worces-

ter to Jeremiah Evarts, 24 October 1825, ABCFM. A Cherokee law passed in 1825 extended Cherokee citizenship to the children of white women and Cherokee men, legally resolving the problem that arose from the traditional practice of clan membership conveying tribal ties, but it probably did not quiet social criticism. *Laws of the Cherokee Nation: Adopted by the Council at Various Periods. Printed for the Benefit of the Nation* (Tahlequah, Cherokee Nation: Cherokee Advocate Office, 1852), 57.

74. Ann Paine, Notebook 2, 20 December 1820, ABCFM.

75. Prejudice against such unions may have declined following enactment of the 1825 law. In 1844, John Ross married a white woman.

76. See Ronald N. Satz, *American Indian Policy in the Jacksonian Era* (Lincoln: University of Nebraska Press, 1975).

77. Jackson to Col. Robert Butler, 5 September 1816, *Correspondence of Andrew Jackson,* 2: 259.

78. U.S. Commissioners to Secretary Graham, 8 July 1817, *Correspondence of Andrew Jackson,* 2: 300.

79. Jackson to Butler, 21 June 1817, *Correspondence of Andrew Jackson,* 2: 299.

80. For an excellent essay on Cherokee chief John Ross and attempts by the United States to discredit him, see Mary Young, "John Ross: Cherokee Chief and Defender of the Nation," in *The Human Tradition in Antebellum America,* ed. Michael A. Morrison (Wilmington, Del.: Scholarly Resources, 2000), 115–30.

81. *Missionary Herald,* July 1818, 339.

82. U.S. Commissioners to Secretary Graham, 8 July 1817, *Correspondence of Andrew Jackson,* 2: 303.

83. Jackson to Butler, 21 June 1817, *Correspondence of Andrew Jackson,* 2: 299.

84. U.S. Commissioners to Secretary Graham, 8 July 1817, *Correspondence of Andrew Jackson,* 2: 300, 304.

85. Lumpkin, *Removal of Cherokee,* 77.

86. U.S. Commissioners to Secretary Graham, 8 July 1817, *Correspondence of Andrew Jackson,* 2: 304.

87. Lumpkin, *Removal of Cherokee,* 78.

88. See Angie Debo, *And Still the Waters Run: The Betrayal of the Five Civ-*

ilized Tribes (1940; reprint, Princeton: Princeton University Press, 1972), especially chapters 1 and 2.

89. Ibid., xiii, 6.

90. U. B. Phillips, "The Central Theme of Southern History," *American Historical Review* 34 (1928): 30–43.

91. U. B. Phillips, *American Negro Slavery: A Survey of the Supply, Employment and Control of Negro Labor as Determined by the Plantation Régime* (New York, London: D. Appleton and Company, 1918); U. B. Phillips, *Life and Labor in the Old South* (Boston: Little, Brown, 1929).

92. U. B. Phillips, "Georgia and State Rights: A Study of the Political History of Georgia from the Revolution to the Civil War with Particular Regard to Federal Relations," *Annual Report of the American Historical Association for the Year 1901* (Washington, D.C.: Government Printing Office, 1902), 2:70. This study, Phillips's doctoral dissertation at Columbia University, won the Justin Winsor Prize of the AHA.

93. Angie Debo, *The Rise and Fall of the Choctaw Republic* (Norman: University of Oklahoma Press, 1934), 77.

94. Angie Debo, *The Road to Disappearance: A History of the Creek Indians* (Norman: University of Oklahoma Press, 1941), 84, 94.

95. Henry Thompson Malone, *Cherokees of the Old South: A People in Transition* (Athens: University of Georgia Press, 1956), 53, 183–84.

96. Gibson, *Chickasaws,* 80–81, 142.

97. McLoughlin, "Accepting Christianity, 1839–1860," in *The Cherokees and Christianity, 1794–1870* (Athens: University of Georgia Press, 1994), 189–90.

98. Claudio Saunt, *A New Order of Things: Property, Power, and the Transformation of the Creek Indians, 1733–1816* (Cambridge: Cambridge University Press, 1999), 2–3.

99. In addition to McLoughlin and Saunt, recent works by Joel Martin, Duane Champagne, and Clara Sue Kidwell, cited previously in this volume, use the language of blood. Champagne's racial analysis is particularly surprising since he recognized that "some traders strategically married into the lineages of local chiefs in order to enhance their trade possibilities and that their children often stood in line for positions of authority and political leadership" (*Social Order,* 54). Martin uses "*métis*" and Saunt "*mes-*

tizo" rather than "mixed blood," perhaps because they sound less racist, but those terms commonly refer to specific categories of persons in the French and Spanish empires whose circumstances differed culturally, socially, legally, and historically from "mixed bloods" in the Southeast.

100. Melissa L. Meyer, *The White Earth Tragedy: Ethnicity and Dispossession at a Minnesota Anishinaabe Reservation, 1889–1920* (Lincoln: University of Nebraska Press, 1994).

Index

Ward, Bryan, 24
Ward, Nancy, 24
Washington, D.C., 85
Washington, George, 50–51
Watts, John, 41–42, 61; parents of, 24
wealth, 49–51, 57–66, 78, 87–89, 95–96, 101
Weatherford, Sehoy McPherson Taitt, 59
Weatherford, William, 44, 46, 68
Wedderburne, David, 11
White Captain, 24

White Earth Anishinaabe Reservation (Minn.), 101–2
Wolf, Janey, 62
Wolf King, 40
women, 7; Indian, 10, 15–23, 30, 63–64, 78, 82, 102; white 8–9, 85–86, 94–95, 125–26 (n. 73)

Yamacraws, 40, 113 (n. 2)
Yamassees, 83
Yamassee War, 110 (n. 74)
Yemassee: A Romance of Carolina, The, 83–84
Young Wolf, 62, 92–93